THE
BRITISH
LANDSCAPE

The
BRITISH
LANDSCAPE

Through the eyes of the great artists

RICHARD HUMPHREYS

IN ASSOCIATION WITH
THE TATE GALLERY

HAMLYN

Author's note
I should like to thank the Publications, Photographic and Technical
Services Departments of the Tate Gallery for all their help and efforts
on my behalf.
I should also like to thank my wife Cat, who not only typed the text
from my chaotic manuscript but also made many useful suggestions
about its style and content. Finally I should mention my daughter
Olivia who forgave me my frequent absences while working on the
book on the understanding her name would appear somewhere in it!

Editor: Lesley McOwan
Art Editor: Ursula Dawson
Design: Hazel Edington
Production: Garry Lewis
Picture Research: Christina Weir and Emily Hedges
Maps: Vali Herzer

This edition published in 1990 by
The Hamlyn Publishing Group Limited,
part of Reed International Books,
Michelin House, 81 Fulham Road,
London SW3 6RB

ISBN 0 600 57152 1

Produced by Mandarin Offset
Printed and bound in Hong Kong

TITLE PAGE ILLUSTRATION: *Llyn Treweryn* by Augustus John (1912)
Oil on panel

CONTENTS

WESTERN ISLES

SCOTLAND

62

61

Aberdeen

60

Dundee

Perth

59

58

Edinburgh

Glasgow

57

56

54

NORTH SEA

53

55

Newcastle upon Tyne

Carlisle

52

51

50

49

ISLE OF MAN

THE NORTH
OF ENGLAND

48

Lancaster

York

IRISH SEA

46

Leeds

42

47

45

Manchester

Liverpool

43

44

30

32

33

Derby

Nottingham

26

31

Leicester

27

17

Norwich

29

28

EAST ANGLIA

WALES

39

23

24

25

18

Cambridge

16

Ipswich

38

THE HEART
OF ENGLAND

19

20

13

15

Swansea

37

36

34

22

Oxford

21

Cardiff

35

Bristol

5

12

14

4

6

THE SOUTH-EAST

11

7

10

Dover

THE SOUTH-WEST

8

9

2

Exeter

3

ISLE OF WIGHT

1

Plymouth

THE CHANNEL

THE SOUTH-WEST
1 Cornwall
2 Devon
3 Dorset
4 Somerset
5 Avon
6 Wiltshire

THE SOUTH-EAST
7 Hampshire
8 West Sussex
9 East Sussex
10 Kent
11 Surrey
12 Berkshire
13 Hertfordshire
14 Greater London

EAST ANGLIA
15 Essex
16 Suffolk
17 Norfolk
18 Cambridgeshire

THE HEART OF ENGLAND
19 Bedfordshire
20 Buckinghamshire
21 Oxfordshire
22 Gloucestershire
23 Hereford and Worcester
24 Warwickshire
25 Northamptonshire
26 Lincolnshire
27 Leicestershire
28 West Midlands
29 Shropshire
30 Cheshire
31 Staffordshire
32 Derbyshire
33 Nottinghamshire

WALES
34 Gwent
35 South Glamorgan
36 Mid Glamorgan
37 West Glamorgan
38 Dyfed
39 Powys
40 Gwynedd
41 Clwyd

THE NORTH OF ENGLAND
42 Humberside
43 South Yorkshire
44 Greater Manchester
45 Merseyside
46 Lancashire
47 West Yorkshire
48 North Yorkshire
49 Cleveland
50 Durham
51 Cumbria
52 Tyne and Wear
53 Northumberland

SCOTLAND
54 Borders
55 Dumfries and Galloway
56 Strathclyde
57 Lothian
58 Central
59 Fife
60 Tayside
61 Grampian
62 Highland

INTRODUCTION

Since the seventeenth century painters have responded to the great variety of Britain's landscape and in doing so have contributed to our awareness of its significant characteristics. A landscape is always affected by human intervention, whether from farming, forestry or the designs of a landscape gardener, and artists have played a part in this process of manipulation. As the images in this book show, artists have painted almost every conceivable part of Britain and have adopted an enormous range of techniques and styles in doing so. These differences of subject, method and purpose reflect not only the artists' individual preferences but also the wider historical and cultural contexts in which they lived and worked.

In many cases during the earlier periods covered by this book the artist's personal interest in the landscape was in fact hardly an issue. The topographical perspective, showing a bird's-eye view of a great country house set in magnificent grounds, was popular in the late seventeenth century, while the classical landscape (an approach which gives an Italian flavour to the British scene) dominated much of the eighteenth century. Both types of image were largely the product of a very particular aristocratic taste, and conformed to a sense of power and ownership which were the sole preserve of the landed elite. That such images became popular beyond the social sphere of the patrons for whom they were produced testifies to the influence the ruling classes exerted on those further down the social scale.

By the later eighteenth century, landscape painting begins to rival portraiture in popularity. One important factor affecting this growth in interest was the Industrial Revolution. The power of the landed class was eroded as a dynamic middle class, rooted in the new industrial and commercial society, came to prominence. This naturally led to new tastes and new demands on artists, and was accompanied by a rapid increase in the number and types of artists. Today's art world, with its public institutions, journals, dealers, critics, and so on, had its origins in this period. Artists now provided images for a largely urban clientele who had a great variety of needs and interests.

One persistent taste, however, was for landscape painting. This is not surprising, as the wealth afforded by the new urban lifestyle was accompanied by feelings of loss and nostalgia for the beauty and simplicity of the countryside.

The tourist trade in Britain also had its roots in this period (Thomas Cook organized his first excursion in 1841) and produced an ever-increasing supply of guide books. These were not only practical and informative guides to particular parts of Britain but also stressed the aesthetic pleasure to be enjoyed by observing the landscape in particular ways, or from particular viewpoints. The use of adjectives like 'beautiful', 'picturesque' and 'sublime' to describe the landscape owes as much to this tourist boom as to the writings of the art critics and art historians of the time. One thing is quite clear from all this obsession with the landscape – the average nineteenth century landscape enthusiast was looking for escape from the grim realities of urban life and from a rural landscape closer to home which, in many cases, was far from the beautiful ideal.

Another feature of the tourist guide book was its frequent emphasis upon the particularly national characteristics of the landscape. People began to see in Britain's 'green and pleasant land' a reflection of their identity and of the nation's destiny. It is a fascinating fact that the 'golden age' of landscape painting coincided with the turmoil of Britain's wars with Napoleonic France and several of the paintings in this book reflect the patriotism of the period.

Even one hundred and fifty years later the powerful feelings generated by those troubled times have left their mark on our image of the landscape. Since the days of Constable and Turner, artists have produced works, with increasing freedom of expression, which present their chosen scenery as mysterious, protective, dangerous, nurturing, timeless and yet constantly changing. The magnificent heritage of British landscape art is both a tribute to the genius of the nation's artists and a record of our rich cultural and historical tradition. Above all, however, it is a reminder of the beautiful and evocative scenery which has served as inspiration to so many great painters.

THE
SOUTH-WEST

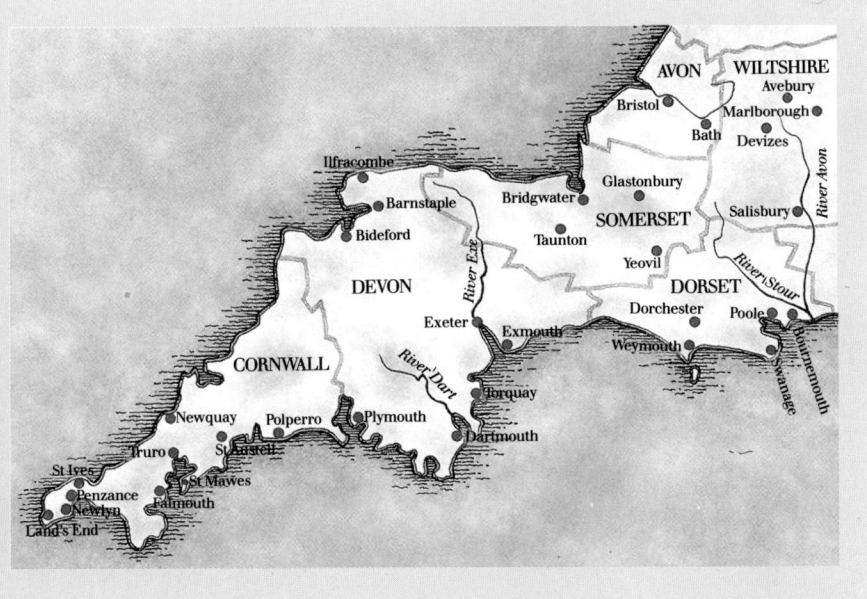

*LEFT: Polperro in Cornwall was home for a time for Oskar
Kokoschka the exiled Austrian artist and the setting for*
The Crab *1939-40 (page 25)*

LANDSCAPES IN MINIATURE

Thomas Gainsborough had a peculiar practice of modelling miniature landscapes in his studio, which then formed the bases of his oil paintings. Uvedale Price, who later became famous as a writer on the 'picturesque', remembers in the 1760s making 'frequent excursions with him into the country' and that the artist 'used to bring home roots, stones, and mosses, from which he formed and then studied foregrounds in miniature'. These models seem to have served as springboards for inspiration and allowed him to invent freely without concern for specific detail: one writer remembered watching Gainsborough in Bath make his models on a small folding oak table kept under his kitchen dresser. 'He would place cork or coal for his foregrounds, make middle grounds of sand and clay, bushes of mosses and lichens, and set up distant woods of brocoli.' The practice has some affinity with the artist Alexander Cozens's famous 'ink-blot' method of landscape composition, publicized in a pamphlet of 1785. A brush filled with ink was allowed to wander at random over the paper, leaving a 'blot' which suggested a landscape image.

THOMAS GAINSBOROUGH
Sunset: Carthorses drinking at a stream
c.1760 Oil on canvas
143.5 × 153.7 cm
56½ × 60½ in
A family travelling home pause to let their horses quench their thirst. The loose brushwork and melancholy sunset glow, highlighted with touches of pink and yellow, show the change in the artist's work during the period he moved to Bath.

The South-west has some of the most varied and beautiful landscape in Britain and its superb coastline and frequently fine weather attract hundreds of thousands of tourists each year. It is an area where artists have not only worked but also settled. In the late eighteenth century the fashionable city of Bath was the home of Thomas Gainsborough for fifteen years, while in the early years of the following century Bristol, which could boast a thriving artistic community as well as ravishing surrounding countryside, attracted Francis Danby, who painted some of his finest landscapes while living there. Newlyn in Cornwall became an important painters' colony in the 1880s, eventually being superseded by St Ives to the north in the first few decades of this century. While St Ives has dominated as the South-west's main artistic centre for the last fifty years or so, Wiltshire and Dorset have also attracted many of the finest painters, including Augustus John and Paul Nash.

GAINSBOROUGH AND PORTRAITURE

Gainsborough worked in Bath between 1759 and 1774, having spent the 1750s painting portraits in Suffolk. Portraiture was also his main business in Bath which, as a fashionable spa for the upper classes, provided a large amount of lucrative work. Gainsborough's success was immediate and spectacular. Although his already considerable talents blossomed in remarkable fashion as he responded to the gaiety of high-life in Bath, Gainsborough, as ever, found most of his clients a bore. There were few noblemen he cared 'a farthing for, or would wear out a pair of shoes in seeking after; long-headed cunning people, and rich fools are so plentiful in our country that I don't fear getting now & then a face to paint for Bread.'

At the end of the aristocratic season in Bath Gainsborough would ride out on horseback into the West Country and sketch the landscape. His favourite sites around Bath were said to be the woods at Claverton and Warleigh and the area around Shockerwick, the seat of his friend Walter Wiltshire, who lent him one of his grey horses for his sketching rides. Many of Gainsborough's later painted landscapes are derived from these sketches made out-of-doors and, as with his earlier views, are imaginary images rather than ones faithful to the landscape. The general characteristics and feel of the countryside are evident but a particular site is rarely identifiable.

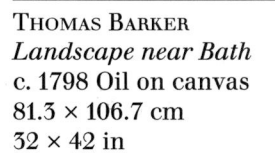

THOMAS BARKER
Landscape near Bath
c. 1798 Oil on canvas
81.3 × 106.7 cm
32 × 42 in

Gainsborough's approach to landscape signifies a Romantic belief in the power of the mind and imagination over observation. For Gainsborough, the invention of his landscapes seems almost to have been a therapeutic exercise in psychological escape. The frequently warm feeling of his pastoral fantasies no doubt derives in part from the circumstances of their production. Uvedale Price wrote,

He loved to sit by the side of his wife during the evenings, and make sketches of whatever occurred to his fancy, all of which he threw below the table, save such as were more than commonly happy, and those were preserved, and either finished as sketches or expanded in paintings.

This domestic origin endorses Constable's reaction to Gainsborough's landscapes as 'soothing, tender, and affecting'.

JOHN CONSTABLE
Salisbury Cathedral from the Meadows
c. 1830 Oil on canvas
36.5 × 51.1 cm
14⅜ × 20⅛ in

One painter influenced by Gainsborough was Thomas Barker of Bath. Barker was immensely successful as a painter of landscape and was a regular exhibitor at the Royal Academy and the British Institution. His debt to Gainsborough and to Richard Wilson (see pages 142–143) is evident in *Landscape near Bath* (c. 1798), which probably shows Hampton Rocks near Bath from a viewpoint near the rocky outcrop known as the Devil's Table. As with many painters of this period, Barker presents a British view in the idealized format of a classical painting, with its succession of planes leading the eye to a distant horizon. The broad composition is carefully balanced and enlivened by figures, trees and rocks which help the eye towards a clump of trees in the centre distance.

JOHN CONSTABLE

Constable made a number of trips to the Southwest, when visiting his friend John Fisher who was archdeacon at Salisbury Cathedral.

Some of Constable's most famous works are views of Salisbury Cathedral. He made two important visits there in 1829, when he developed a series of drawings in a large sketchbook which, like the Tate Gallery's *Salisbury Cathedral from the Meadows,* are almost certainly studies towards his last major painting of the cathedral, exhibited in 1831, and which is now held in a private collection. This oil sketch has traces of squaring-up (squaring-up is a process whereby the preliminary drawings or sketches for a painting are scaled and marked on the canvas, as a guide for the finished work) and other pencil marks under the paint which further suggest its relationship to the final painting. As in the exhibited work, Constable introduces St Thomas's church on the left (a physical impossibility from the viewpoint taken), and a wagon pulled by a team of three horses.

Two important differences between the Tate's painting and the final version are the lack of a rainbow in the Tate's painting and the inclusion in it of a man and dog crossing the bridge on the right. In his 1823 painting of the cathedral Constable had included the bishop and his wife and perhaps he thought it would be a nice touch to include his friend the archdeacon in this version. Only the dog remains in the exhibited painting, however, echoing similar canine presences in *The Haywain* and *Hadleigh Castle.* There is little doubt that the stormy weather surrounding Salisbury Cathedral is a reference to the anxiety felt by both Constable and Fisher about the state of the Church of England in an age of dramatic change. In these years just before the great Reform Bill of 1832, conservatives such as Constable believed the Church stood between social order and anarchy. Fisher had expressed the view earlier in the 1820s that 'by protecting and supporting a particular Church we avail ourselves of all the advantages which a civil government must acquire from religion.'

THE BRISTOL SCHOOL

Bristol became an important centre for art in the early nineteenth century and after 1810 a circle of artists around the painter Edward Bird began to meet in order to sketch and to discuss art. This group became known as the Bristol School and included one artist of outstanding

THE COUNTRYSIDE AROUND BATH

By the late eighteenth century the countryside around Bath was universally recognized as being of outstanding picturesque beauty, as these words by the painter Benjamin West, recorded by the painter and diarist Joseph Farington in 1807, testify,

> Take Bath and twenty miles round it and there is not in the world anything superior to it. Rocks of the finest forms for a painter that he had ever seen, large square forms. Quarrys worked out now most picturesque, distances the most beautiful – roads with the occasional pools and streams of water

The countryside around Bath inspired some of the greatest British landscape painters, including Thomas Gainsborough and John Constable

falling from the hills. . . Strangely enough, although Bath proved popular with artists on account of its wealthy and constantly changing population, it was unable, as Norwich and other provincial centres had been able, to sustain an annual exhibition. Barker's friend and patron Sir William Cockburn told Farington in 1811 that,

> there no longer remained any hope of keeping up an Annual Bath Exhibition . . . the people resident in that city shewing no disposition to visit it so as to produce Door-money enough for its support.

By the 1820s Bath was no longer a fashionable spot; John Fisher, archdeacon at Salisbury Cathedral and nephew of the bishop there, wrote to his close friend, John Constable in 1824, agreeing with Constable's view that 'there is no art . . . out of London' and telling of the impossibility of buying a decent landscape engraving in the city of Bath.

FRANCIS DANBY
Children by a Brook
c. 1822 Oil on canvas
34 × 46 cm
13⅜ × 18⅛ in
Francis Danby was born in Ireland and moved to England in 1813, settling in Bristol where he lived until 1824. Stapleton, on the River Frome was a popular spot with Danby and Children by a Brook is derived from studies of the area. The painting is a celebration of the innocent enchantment of childhood. Nature and innocence were to become common linked themes in Victorian painting and here Danby creates an almost womb-like space to suggest calm and nurture.

J. M. W. TURNER
Crossing the Brook
c. 1815 Oil on canvas
193 × 165.11 cm
76 × 65 in

J. M. W. TURNER
*St Mawes at the
Pilchard Season*
1812 Oil on canvas
91.1 × 120.6 cm
35⅞ × 47½ in

talent: Francis Danby, who lived in the city be-tween 1817 and 1824. Although, as with the artists of the contemporaneous Norwich School, the Bristol artists found inspiration in their im-mediate vicinity, there was a strong tendency in their work towards fantasy.

J. M. W. TURNER

In the early eighteenth century there was also a tendency among certain artists to manipulate a recognizable site in the interests of some liter-ary or sentimental impulse. This can be seen to some extent in Turner's very large painting of a bridge on the River Wear, *Crossing the Brook*, exhibited in 1815 and produced from sketches made during a tour of Devon in 1813. The painter Charles Eastlake was quite clear about the exact scene chosen by Turner,

> *The bridge ... is Calstock Bridge;
> some mining works are indicated in
> the middle distance. The extreme
> distance extends to the mouth of the
> Tamar, the harbour of Hamoaze, the
> hills of Mount Edgecumbe, and those*

> *on the opposite side of Plymouth
> Sound. The whole scene is extremely
> faithful.*

While this may be the case, it is also true that, following the example of Richard Wilson (see page 143), Turner has painted a scene in the Italianate style of Claude Lorraine. The effect of this approach is to give the view a timeless air evoking the Mediterranean landscape admired by contemporary taste. The painting did not sell, however, and this may have been because of the poor opinion of it expressed by the in-fluential painter, collector and patron, Sir George Beaumont. He attacked it for consisting of a 'pea-green insipidity'.

In great contrast to the classicizing form of *Crossing the Brook* is Turner's *St Mawes at the Pilchard Season,* which shows St Mawes on Fal-mouth harbour, with Pendennis Castle shim-mering in the distance. It is probably the result of a visit the artist made to Cornwall in the sum-mer of 1811 in connection with work for W. B. Cooke's *Picturesque Views of the Southern Coast of England,* published between 1814 and 1826. The painting is dominated by hustle and bustle after the arrival of the fishing fleet, and the foreground is alive with gleaming fish. This is a working landscape dominated by humans and the reality of their economic existence. Turner is alert to the confusion yet sense of purpose in the scene and he relegates the natural and architectural elements to what is nevertheless an important background function.

JOHN WILLIAM INCHBOLD

In the middle of the nineteenth century a shift towards a highly precise kind of naturalism can be discerned which marks a great change in taste. Much of this can be attributed to a growing faith in the truths offered by science for understanding the natural world. The Pre-Raphaelites and in particular their supporter, the critic John Ruskin, believed that a metic-

ABOVE: Calstock Bridge over the River Wear in Devon – featured in J.M.W. Turner's Crossing the Brook *c. 1815.*

ulous imitation of nature supplied the artist with all he needed. This faith in direct observation and painstaking depiction can be found in John William Inchbold's *The Moorland (Dewar-Stone, Dartmoor)* (1854), which shows a famous beauty spot near Plymouth. The artist paints the foreground detail with an almost photographic accuracy and a concern for the minute varieties of colour under a wide evening sky. It was this

kind of meticulous attention to naturalistic detail which made Ruskin an admirer of Inchbold's painting in the 1850s.

NEWLYN

Cornwall was first discovered by artists in the early nineteenth century. Joseph Farington toured there in 1809 and Turner in 1811, but its unique and extremely harsh character, considered by natives and outsiders alike as very un-English, made it almost totally resistant to full-scale tourism and settlement until late in the century.

Tennyson travelled to Tintagel Castle in 1860, in search of Arthurian atmosphere, and others soon began to appreciate the romantic legends surrounding ancient 'Cornubia'. In 1876 it became possible to travel from London to Penzance by train in what was for those times, a re-

markable ten and a half hours; Cornwall was now, without doubt, fully open to discovery.

Newlyn, on the south Penwith coast, was the first important site for painters in the nineteenth century. The main industry there was fishing, and the people lived in small, brightly painted cottages attractively decorated with flowers and vines.

The lives of those who lived in Newlyn were constantly threatened by tragedy and poverty and, most disasterous of all, was the ever pre-

JOHN WILLIAM INCHBOLD
The Moorland (Dewar-Stone, Dartmoor)
1854 Oil on canvas
35.6 × 53.3 cm
14 × 21 in

THE ATTRACTIONS OF CORNWALL

Newlyn became an artists' colony in the late nineteenth-century

For many artists, Cornish fishing villages such as Newlyn and St Ives were British counterparts to the towns and villages of Brittany which had been colonized by French painters in the 1870s and 1880s. It was not just the landscapes and seascapes that attracted the artists, nor even the mythical Celtic associations, but also the simple, pre-industrial lives of the inhabitants. 'Here every corner was a picture, and, more important from the point of view of the figure-painter, the people seemed to fall naturally into their places, and to harmonise with their surroundings,' wrote the painter Stanhope Forbes of Newlyn. Artists like Forbes and Walter Langley had lived in Brittany for a number of years and upon their return to Great Britain had subsequently moved to 'wild', usually coastal sites to establish their own colonies.

sent danger that the mackerel season would fail which could leave most of the town's population destitute.

The streets of Newlyn were cobbled and there was a chaotic maze of courts and alleyways surrounded by lofts, cellars and 'gearns', where all kinds of fishing gear was dumped and maintained.

The dominant artistic figure in Newlyn was Stanhope Forbes, who arrived at the village in 1884, two years after Walter Langley had settled there. Forbes brought with him a style influenced by the French painter Jules Bastien-Lepage, whom he described as 'the greatest artist of our age'. Bastien-Lepage was the advocate of a disciplined *plein-air* (open-air) painting characterized by an uncompromising realism and a distinctive technique in which the paint is applied in tight diagonal strokes with a flat-ended brush. This was known as the 'square brush' technique and led to an emphasis on tone which gives the paintings a very particular atmosphere.

The emphasis in Newlyn on working out of doors to achieve a direct realism was sardonically referred to by the Irish painter Norman Garstin when he said, 'your work cannot really be good unless you have caught a cold doing it'. Garstin also asserted that the Newlyn artists sought in their work to 'represent not only the man but, as it were, his very atmosphere, and not only his surroundings but his surroundings under certain specific conditions'.

The result was the kind of powerful image Frank Bramley achieved in his *A Hopeless*

Dawn, shown at the Royal Academy in 1888. A young wife collapses on the lap of an old woman in a fishing cottage, the stormy sea and sky seen through the window telling us that her husband has been lost at sea. It was the women of the fishing communities, of course, who suffered the brunt of tragedies as shown in *A Hopeless Dawn* and thus became such poignant figures for the painters. Symbolism underlines the tragedy: in the dark, on a wall to the right, a print after Raphael's cartoon of *Christ giving the Keys to St Peter*; an open Bible in front of the old woman; and, left on the window-sill, a candle which has just flickered out. Bramley quoted a passage from Ruskin in the Royal Academy catalogue, giving the picture a typically Victorian religious and moral significance,

> *Human effort and sorrow going on*
> *perpetually from age to age; waves*
> *rolling for ever and winds moaning,*
> *and faithful hearts wasting and*
> *sickening for ever, and brave lives*
> *dashed away about the rattling*
> *beach like weeds for ever; and still at*
> *the helm of every lonely boat, through*
> *starless night and hopeless dawn, His*
> *hand, who spreads the fisher's net*
> *over the dust of the Sidonian palaces,*
> *and gave unto the fisher's hand the*
> *keys of the kingdom of heaven.*

The grimness of the situation is above all evoked by Bramley's skilful rendering of the subtle grey tones of the early morning light. The painting was produced in a tiny ceiling-lit studio in a two-roomed cottage. Stanhope Forbes recalled that Bramley 'certainly had the right atmosphere for his subject for his models were real fisherfolk, and the window of the cottage in which the two women sit waiting for the dawn almost looked over the bay'.

LAURA KNIGHT

Harold and Laura Knight moved to Cornwall in 1910, staying first in Newlyn and making frequent visits to Lamorna where Laura painted some of her finest works. She caused a storm among the locals by using nude male and female models from London in the open air. Complaints were made to Colonel Paynter, who

FRANK BRAMLEY
A Hopeless Dawn
1888 Oil on canvas
122.6 × 167.6 cm
48¼ × 66 in

owned most of the land along this stretch of the coast, but he however, fully supported Knight. In 1912 the Knights moved to Oakhill, a house near Lamorna converted for them by Paynter, where they lived until 1918.

It was here between 1916 and 1920 that Laura painted *Spring,* one of her most beautiful images which shows the countryside around Lamorna, although the original idea came to the artist when she was in Staithes in Yorkshire many years earlier. Knight's art, with its strong impressionist colour, is usually a kind of hymn to the joys of natural life outdoors, and is very much of its time in its Bohemian cult of youth and nature worship. The two models in the painting are Ella and Charles Napier, and their surroundings, painted with a Pre-Raphaelite intensity, form an ironic contrast to the period in which they were living – the middle of the First World War. Knight recalled that

> *at that time it was against the law to paint out of doors anywhere near the Cornish coast. And to get the material I needed, here and there, I had to lie on my stomach under a gorse or any other convenient bush,*

> *in dread of being taken off to prison, to make a line or two in a sketch book, memorise – rush back into my studio and paint.*

The dream-like atmosphere of the painting reflects the circumstances in which it was made and also the artist's need to construct an ideal natural world, as it were, against the fact of war.

ST IVES

On the other side of the Penwith peninsula from Newlyn is the fishing village of St Ives. With its dramatic granite setting, sheltered harbour, fishlofts, alleyways and whitewashed cob walls, St Ives, like Newlyn, became a favourite spot for artists. J. A. M. Whistler and Walter Sickert stayed there for a few months in the winter of 1883-4 and by the turn of the century St Ives closely rivalled Newlyn in its popularity. Newlyn, in fact, had been remodelled as a working port by 1900 and had lost much of its original charm and attraction, while St Ives, which in effect began to stagnate economically, remained a picturesque village of great appeal to a wide range of artists. Studios were rapidly converted

DAME LAURA KNIGHT
Spring
1916-20 Oil on canvas
152.4 × 182.9 cm
60 × 72 in

SIR MATTHEW SMITH
Cornish Church
1920 Oil on canvas
53.3 × 64.8 cm
21 × 25½ in

from sail lofts and cheaply available cottages were taken along Porthmeor Beach. Harewood Robinson, the author of *Historical Sketches of St Ives* (1896), observed . . .

> *large skylights appeared everywhere among the grey roofs of the old town; by the enterprise of the townspeople studios were built, some of imposing size, and St Ives took its place as a world-known centre of art work.*

Most of the artists in St Ives were fairly traditional in their approach and affiliated to the numerous societies and art clubs. Artists from London still visited St Ives in the 1920s and painted the local landscape, while others, such as Matthew Smith, visited sites in Cornwall, attracted by the area's bleak beauty.

Smith's *Cornish Church* was painted in the winter of 1920 and shows the church at St Columb Major, inland from Newquay, in sombre expressionist colours against an extraordinary black sky. Matthew Smith, who had a deeply profound love of Brittany, responded powerfully to the dark granite buildings of the village and painted a series of works which in their use of flat areas of colour show the influence of the French painters Paul Gauguin and Henri Matisse.

St Ives is best known as the home of two generations of modernist painters who worked there between the late 1930s and the mid-1960s. The story of this association of St Ives with modernism has an intriguing beginning,

> *On the way back from Porthmeor Beach we passed an open door in Back Road West and through it saw some paintings of ships and houses on odd pieces of paper and cardboard nailed up all over the wall, with particularly large nails through the smaller ones. We knocked on the door and inside found Wallis, and the paintings we got from him were among the first he made.*

These are the words of the painter Ben Nicholson, recalling how he and Christopher Wood by chance came across the 'primitive' paintings of Alfred Wallis in 1928.

Wallis, who had once been a fisherman, ran a marine and rag-and-bone store in St Ives. When

his wife died in the early 1920s he began to paint, 'for company', on irregular-shaped bits of cardboard given to him by the local grocer and on bits of wood he picked up in the area. His images were made with a limited range of ship's enamel or household paint which he thickly scumbled over blue and green grounds. (scumbling is a technique used to build up the surface of a painting. The artist will drag or skim paint over the work using a palette knife or similar implement.) Wallis is often seen as the British Douanier Rousseau, although his work is far cruder in composition and technique than that of the great French 'naïve' painter. The perspective is primitive in the extreme and the scale quite illogical, giving prominence to the objects most important to Wallis, such as the boats and houses. Wallis either worked to the odd configuration of his cardboard and wood supports as he found them, or cut them to some desired shape. He began to paint when he was about 70 and his images are mostly nostalgic reminiscences.

Nicholson and Wood were fascinated by the simple, bold design and naïve vision of Wallis's paintings: Wood visited Wallis almost every day for three months in 1928-9 and both he and Nicholson at this time painted works which show a sophisticated use of many of the features of the old man's work.

In the summer of 1939 the critic and painter Adrian Stokes invited Nicholson, his wife the

ALFRED WALLIS
The Hold House, Port Mear, Square Island, Port Mear Beach
c. 1932 Oil on paper
30.5 × 38.7 cm
12 × 15¼ in

THE SEVEN AND FIVE SOCIETY

Ben Nicholson 1894-1982

Christopher Wood 1901-30

The artists Ben Nicholson and Christopher Wood were both members of the London-based Seven and Five Society, which favoured a child-like quality in art. The fashion for 'naïve' art was at its peak in the 1920s and, as the critic Charles Harrison has pointed out, 'there was a tendency during the mid-twenties to regard art as an activity requiring a form of artlessness.' This notion of innocence required the rejection of obvious technical sophistication and Nicholson was particularly impressed by Wallis's 'using the materials nearest to hand', which 'is the motive and method of the first creative artist'. During the 1930s Nicholson carved his famous abstract white reliefs out of old table-tops picked up in junk shops, very much in keeping with such views.

BEN NICHOLSON
St Ives, Cornwall
1943-5 Oil on board
40.6 × 50.2 cm
16 × 19¾ in

sculptress Barbara Hepworth and their children to stay with him, and the visitors stayed in Cornwall for the whole of the war, eventually settling near Carbis Bay. Nicholson made many beautiful line drawings and paintings of the west Cornish landscape and of buildings in and around St Ives during the 1940s; in his Porthmeor studio, he made large semi-abstract pieces based on still-life and landscape arrangements. His view of St Ives harbour was painted in 1943, one of his first landscapes for thirteen years, and shows quite clearly the bay, boats and distant hills as seen through a window. The foreground of the painting is dominated by a still life, reworked in 1945, which sets up a fascinating relationship between the forms of the mugs and the shapes in the landscape. Pale scrubbed colours and a fine varying line were to become characteristic features of

Nicholson's art. The debt to his discovery of Alfred Wallis is still evident in his work in spite of Nicholson's sophistication.

A NEW GENERATION

It was the pre-war pioneers of modernist abstraction, such as Nicholson, Hepworth and John Tunnard, who, through their working presence in Cornwall during and after the war, were to prove such an inspiration to a new generation of experimental artists in St Ives. These younger artists included Bryan Wynter, Peter Lanyon, Patrick Heron and Terry Frost, who took St Ives from being another provincial group of British artists in the tradition of the Norwich and Bristol Schools to acclaim at an international level. Although their work is abstract or semi-abstract and is usually seen in connection with post-war American abstract art, all these artists found inspiration in the same landscape that had attracted Stanhope Forbes and Laura Knight before them.

OSKAR KOKOSCHKA

A number of foreign artists, usually political exiles, moved to Cornwall during the war, including the Russian constructivist sculptor Naum Gabo and the Austrian expressionist painter Oskar Kokoschka. Kokoschka, who had arrived in England in 1938, moved in August 1939 to Polperro, a small fishing village between Fowey and Looe on the south Cornish coast, where he lived in a house on a cliff with magnificent views of the sea.

At the outbreak of the war it was forbidden, for security reasons, to paint or draw out of doors and Kokoschka was forced to work from memory in his studio. He made a series of watercolours of the local scenery before embarking on a number of oil paintings including *The Crab* and *Polperro II*. Both works show Kokoschka's hyperactive and ferocious expressionist style, in which the sky, cliffs and sea of the landscape become an agitated surface of rich and luxurious paint. The effect is wholly un-English, particularly in *The Crab*, where an enormous crustacean monster towers over the harbour and seems to threaten a small human figure swimming with difficulty towards the pier. Kokoschka, who was also a poet and playwright, produced an art which was frequently literary and loaded with meaning and this painting is, according to the artist's friend Edward Beddington-Behrens, a political allegory. The crab represents Neville Chamberlain,

OSKAR KOKOSCHKA
The Crab
1939-40 Oil on canvas
63.4 × 76.2 cm
25 × 30 in

PETER LANYON
Porthleven
1951 Oil on board
244.5 × 121.9 cm
96¼ × 48 in
*Porthleven is a fishing port,
on Mount's Bay across the*
peninsula to the south of St.
Ives. Lanyon's painting was
commissioned in 1950 for
an Arts Council exhibition
the following year.

British Prime Minister until 1940, who 'would only have to put out one claw to save [the human figure] from drowning, but remains aloof.' The swimmer represents Czechoslovakia, of which Kokoschka, though Austrian born, held citizenship, due to the fact that his father was born there. Kokoschka's bitterness at the behaviour of all political leaders is also expressed in his cryptic inscription on the back of *Polperro II*: '30 years of an/emigrants/artistic wisdom/An artist's signature/remains – but leaders/of states bloom & fall/All? Why? –/How an artist lives!/gives!' Kokoschka must have been even more displeased when he was forced to leave Polperro in the summer of 1940: the whole of the southern coastline was declared a defence area from which all foreign nationals were excluded.

AUGUSTUS JOHN
Lyric Fantasy/The Blue Lake
1910-15 Oil and drawing on canvas
233.7 × 469.9 cm
92 × 185 in

WILTSHIRE AND DORSET

Wiltshire and Dorset have landscapes whose character is very much associated with the mysteries of prehistory. Ancient burial sites, chalk carvings and megalithic stones abound in these dramatic downlands, from Avebury in the north, across the Salisbury Plain to the splendid coastline stretching west from Poole to Lyme Regis. Something of the strange timelessness of this particular landscape was captured in Thomas Hardy's description of the area around Wareham in Dorset: 'A Face on which Time makes but Little Impression'.

The human face, and body, seem to lie within the downs and plains overcast, as Paul Nash wrote, 'by the burden of [their] extraordinary inheritance'. So here we have a sense of the landscape as a setting for the human drama of which, in some indefinable way, it is an image. Three artists in particular this century looked for new ways of expressing this: Augustus John, Paul Nash and David Inshaw.

AUGUSTUS JOHN

Augustus John moved in 1911 from fashionable Chelsea to Alderney Manor in Parkstone, near Poole, where he lived with his second wife Dorelia until 1927. The artist Henry Lamb, who had an affair with Dorelia while Augustus amused himself with his countless models, wrote to the writer Lytton Strachey, describing Alderney Manor as 'an amazing place in a vast secluded park of prairies, pine woods, birch woods, dells and moors with a house, cottage and a circular walled garden'.

PAUL NASH
*Equivalents for the
Megaliths*
1935 Oil on canvas
45.7 × 66 cm
18 × 26 in

The Johns were surrounded by their growing family and lived a free, spontaneous life hardly imaginable today. John's *Lyric Fantasy* was painted at Chelsea and Alderney between 1910 and 1915, as part of an unfinished scheme of three large paintings commissioned in 1909 by the publisher Sir Hugh Lane, for his house in Cheyne Walk, Chelsea. The work, unfinished partly because of Lane's death on the *Lusitania* in 1915, reveals John's belief that 'the finest decoration can be produced without any direct reference to visual "Nature" – that is, it will be as it were a natural growth itself. . . .' John drew directly on the canvas with pencil and then painted over this, and his improvisation is quite clearly visible in the shifting figures and *pentimenti* (*pentimento* is a term used to describe the reappearance of earlier underlying painting or drawing when the layer added later becomes transparent, revealing the artist's change of mind). On the right of the work is John's first wife Ida, who died in 1907 and is included presumably in a spiritual capacity; the central figure with the mandolin is Dorelia; the boy with the drum is John's son Pyramus and the other boys are, from left to right, his other sons Caspar, Romilly and Edwin. These family members, and the other figures arranged frieze-like across the canvas, take part in a kind of anarchic ritual in front of a landscape based on the area near Alderney Manor. The painting's alternative title, *Blue Lake,* probably refers to the clay works at nearby Wareham Heath (Hardy's Egdon Heath), although the mountains in the background are pure poetic, or rather painterly licence, evoking a memory of John's native Wales and demonstrating his strongly-held view that 'all imitative art is a bore.' The painting has affinities with similar lyrical visions of the French artists Paul Gauguin and Pierre Puvis de Chavannes, painted in the late nineteenth century.

PAUL NASH

Perhaps the greatest British landscape painter of the twentieth century is Paul Nash. He lived in Swanage, Dorset, between October 1934 and March 1936 while working on the *Shell Guide to Dorset,* for which he wrote an essay and made drawings. For the first few months of his stay Nash lived in Whitecliff Farm in the suburbs of Swanage, and the view from here over Ballard Down towards the sea appears frequently in his works of this period.

In 1929 Nash first began to suffer from the asthma which eventually led to his death. When

RIGHT: The ancient Avebury standing stones provided the inspiration for Paul Nash's Equivalents for the Megaliths *1935*

his condition became serious in 1933 he went to convalesce with a friend, Ruth Clark, in Marlborough, Wiltshire, spending the summer there. He had chosen this area because of his interest in Savernake Forest, where he had painted in the 1920s. It was the prehistoric stones at nearby Avebury, however, which really captured his imagination, along with Stonehenge to the south and the enormous earthworks at Silbury, all set in a landscape he loved above all others. Nash recalled his first visit to Avebury almost as a part of his cure.

> *The great stones were then in their wild state, so to speak. Some were half-covered by the grass, others stood up in cornfields or were entangled and overgrown in the copses, some were buried in the turf. But they were wonderful and disquieting, and as I saw them then, I shall always remember them.*

This description is in sharp contrast to his most important Avebury painting, *Equivalents for the Megaliths* (1935). Here the ancient stones lose their rough shapes and texture and are transformed into geometrical shapes. Nash explained the meaning of the painting in a long and revealing statement written for its first owner, Lance Sieveking,

> *In the fields a few miles north of Marlborough, standing or prone, are the huge stones, remains of the avenue, or the circles of the Temple of Avebury. The appearance of one or more of these megaliths, blotched with ochreish lichens, or livid with the bruises of weathering is sufficiently dramatic in a field of stubble, or in the grass meadows. But it is dramatic in two different ways. These groups are impressive as forms opposed to their surroundings, both by virtue of their actual composition of lines, masses and planes, directions and volume; and in the irrational sense, their suggestion of a super-reality. They are dramatic also as symbols of their antiquity, as hallowed remnants of an almost unknown civilisation.*

Nash went on to explain why he had used mathematical forms, wishing, he said, to avoid too overt a suggestion of the antiquarian or picturesque. He was also at this time committed to an idea of injecting a greater sense of structure into British art, which he felt too often lapsed

THE RURALIST BROTHERHOOD

A 'ruralist' strictly speaking is someone who moves from the town to the country. Peter Blake the former pop artist did this when he moved to Wellow, near Bath, in 1969. In 1975 he formed the 'Brotherhood of Ruralists' with the painter David Inshaw and, later, with Graham Arnold and Graham Ovenden. Country life, Victorian culture and Pre-Raphaelite art were the main enthusiasms of the Brotherhood who were in deliberate reaction to the abstract and conceptual art which was dominant at the time. They held a major touring exhibition in 1981 which was also their swan-song as a group. They were pioneers of the 'return' to figurative art which has been so noticeable in the last ten years. One significant feature of the Ruralists' work is its eroticism which has links with the work of one of their few twentieth century heroes, Stanley Spencer. Like Spencer the Ruralists emphasised physical ecstasy in their paintings, much of it focused in images of naked pubescent girls and young women in landscape settings. In some senses the Ruralists are the liberated, post-1960s heirs of Samuel Palmer and the Ancients who they admire so much.

into a loose impressionism and 'unconscious' imitation of nature. *Equivalents for the Megaliths* thus combines the three central strands of Paul Nash's art in the mid-1930s: the search for a powerful underlying abstract design; the surrealist sense of the dream-like and disquieting; and a profound interest in the historical and imaginative meanings of a specific landscape. Nash's sense of place was obviously informed by the threat of imminent loss. The *Shell Guide to Dorset* was dedicated to 'all those courageous enemies of "development" to whom we owe what is left of England'. These are familiar heart-felt sentiments fifty years later.

DAVID INSHAW

The dream atmosphere of Nash's Wiltshire and Dorset works is of a very different order to that found in the work of the contemporary artist David Inshaw. Both artists, however, shared a deep love of this part of the country. Inshaw said: 'I fell in love with the Downs and the Vale on my first visit. I felt as if history had been condensed to a moment by walking in the landscape about Devizes.'

Inshaw moved to Devizes, near Avebury, in the autumn of 1971. He had been teaching at Bristol Art School and wanted to get away from the stresses of work and the city.

Inshaw's *The Badminton Game* (1972-3) is one of the Tate's most popular pictures. It shows two women, with whom Inshaw was in love, playing badminton in the garden of a large Georgian red-brick house. Behind them tower enormous trees and topiary bushes, while to the right a glimpse of the downs can be seen. The bright blue sky has patches of 'mackerel' cloud, which gives the image a faint sense of antici-

pation and foreboding. There is an uncanny stillness about the scene, as if this were some sort of ghostly coloured photograph.

As Nash had been before him, Inshaw was very interested in photography at this time and was seeking to make a painting which froze time as the camera does, but gave a 'universal, deeper meaning to the moment by composing an instant from a lot of different unrelated moments'. Inshaw saw this effect in his favourite early Renaissance paintings, where the moment held in time seems to contain the 'emotion of all time'. The moment, with the shuttlecock poised in mid-flight and the two young women held in statuesque poses, is a repository for many thoughts and moments, 'happy thoughts as well as sad, full of waking dreams and erotic fancies'. Inshaw remembers being in a state of emotional and physical chaos at the time, due to his love affairs, the men working on his new house in Lansdowne Terrace, Devizes, and the general effects of his move from Bristol, and the painting was thus an attempt to bring some order into his actual and spiritual affairs,

> Everything in the picture is taken from near my house in Devizes and rearranged into its right place. I changed everything I used in the picture in order to increase the mystery and wonder I felt all around me in this magic place.

The sense of place, as in Nash's work, is very strong, even though physical accuracy has been abandoned. Appropriately, Inshaw's original title for the painting was a line from Thomas Hardy's haunting poem *She, to Him* 1866, about the transcience of female beauty: 'Remembering mine the loss is, not the blame'.

DAVID INSHAW
The Badminton Game
1972-3 Oil on canvas
152.4 × 183.5 cm
60 × 72¼ in

THE
SOUTH-EAST

LEFT: *A view of the white horse on White Horse Hill, Berkshire.*
A complete view of this famous prehistoric 'carving' in the
downland chalk can be seen in Eric Ravilious's crisply
executed watercolour, The Vale of the White Horse *c. 1939*
(page 53)

MYLES BIRKET FOSTER
*Lane Scene at
Hambledon*
Exhibited 1862
Watercolour
42.5 × 63.5 cm
16¾ × 25 in
*Myles Birket Foster's work
is characterised by intense
detail achieved through
stippling with tiny brush
strokes using very little
water. His typical imagery
is of sunny, untroubled
country scenes peopled by
children and haymakers.
Hambledon, still a small
village, is a few miles south
of Godalming in Surrey.
Foster rented a cottage
there in 1860 as a residence
for the summer, and it was
from here that he
supervised the building of
his house in Witley.*

The South-east is usually identified with the prosperous middle classes who work in London and live and retire in what have become known as the Home Counties. While there is much truth in this account it ignores the fact that well into this century the area around London was rural landscape with its fair share of poverty and deprivation. Of course the mostly gentle rolling countryside lacks the dramatic scale and sublime power of other areas of Britain and accounts for the rather cosy and re-assuring image that many people have of the South-east.

In a sense, however, the most important factor in considering this particular region is that it surrounds London and, since the rapid growth of the city, has partly become an extension of it. In terms of the ideas that informed people's understanding of the word 'landscape', the South-east is therefore a little problematic. While it undoubtedly boasts some beautiful and varied scenery its proximity to London has mostly made it seem the very antithesis of the natural beauty expected of landscape. The South-east has been compromised by its status as a glorified suburb.

JAN GRIFFIER

Jan Griffier's view of Hampton Court Palace is an early landscape which, to judge by the figures' costumes, was probably painted about 1710. It is a little unusual, although not unique, in its technique, for it is painted in oil on copper. The view is an invention showing the palace from the east, with Windsor Castle on the right and the Banqueting House on the left, flanking it. Such fantasies, called 'caprices' or 'capriccios', were popular at this time, when landscape often served a decorative role. The general view taken is very close to the one in *Britannia Illustrata* (1707-8), a set of engravings after drawings by Leonard Knyff, of the great houses of Britain, showing them from an elevated angle and usually set in magnificent formal gardens. In this painting Griffier, who was born in Amsterdam and moved to England in the 1660s, has given his capriccio a dream-like quality: a view of the Thames (where, incidentally, the artist lived on a yacht for some time) seems to become a romantic reminiscence of the Rhine as well.

Tantalizing questions about this painting, un-fortunately, have no clear answers. Who com-

JAN GRIFFIER, THE ELDER
View of Hampton Court Palace
c. 1710 Oil on copper
38.1 × 50.5 cm
15 × 19⅞ in

BELOW: A present-day view of Hampton Court palace and its magnificent gardens

missioned the work? In what circumstances was it originally hung? For what reason was this particular group of buildings brought together? Who are the figures in the foreground? The lack of answers to these questions leaves us with a mysterious gem of a painting which reminds us how incomplete our grasp of the not-so-distant past often is. One thing we do know about Griffier is that he spent his later years living in a house on Millbank, the stretch of the Thames where the Tate now stands.

GEORGE LAMBERT

George Lambert's *View of Box Hill, Surrey* (1733) shows the Mole Gap and the Mickleham Downs on the left, from Ranmore Common. It is possible that the precise viewpoint is from the former Denbies Carriage Drive. The painting forms a pair with another view of the same location which represents gentlemen picnicking and reading a map on the hillside. In this painting Lambert shows a number of field workers: one is working (a close examination shows his scythe was originally to the left); another sharpens his scythe while talking to a seated woman with a leather ale bottle by her side; and another can be seen carrying a child along a

path through the corn. The centre of the painting is dominated by a gentleman standing above a seated figure at work on a drawing. To their right a man lies by a picnic basket, pointing a little disconsolately at a spilt bottle of wine.

It has been suggested that the three men are engaged in a land survey, although they may be artists. Whatever the case, this is a 'landscape of improvement', like that of Jan Siberechts' view of Henley-on-Thames (see page 104). A wide panoramic view focuses on a great chalky hill and beneath it sets out the main features of the landscape in clear and orderly fashion. People are shown working and studying the landscape in a manner which suggests their control over nature. Lambert was also a theatrical scene painter at Lincoln's Inn and Covent Garden and some of his skills in such work are perhaps evident in the clarity of the composition and the placing of the figures.

GEORGE LAMBERT
View of Box Hill, Surrey
1733 Oil on canvas
90.8 × 184.1 cm
35¾ × 72½ in

JAMES SEYMOUR

James Seymour's *A Kill at Ashdown Park* (1743) was commissioned by Fulwar, 4th Baron Cra-

ven, who is the nearest horseman in the painting, wearing a three-cornered hat. He is shown here with his huntsman and tricolour hounds at the end of a fox-hunt on the Berkshire Downs. In the distance on the left, surrounded by a walled wood, is his seat, Ashdown House, which was built for the first earl in about 1665. On the hills behind the hunting group, a shepherd tends a flock of sheep while two dogs chase a hare. The central interest of the painting, however, is the raising of the fox: the hounds eagerly gather round, one of them leaping up to claim the kill as his own. Around them the members of the hunt, standing or mounted on horseback, watch the scene dispassionately. Dotted around the foreground are the 'sarsens' or sandstone boulders peculiar to the district.

Little is known about Seymour except that, despite a rather dissipated lifestyle, he was one of the most successful sporting painters in the first half of the eighteenth century. His images became widely known during and after his life-

time through the cheap coloured prints published by Carington Bowles. His style is characterized by a firm outline, clear colour and precise detail.

There is a naïve quality to all Seymour's work, which lends it an imaginary feeling. The hills in this painting, Weathercock and Crowberry Tump, are huge bare mounds and the scale and perspective throughout seem uncertain. Seymour's main concern is to create a vivid and factually accurate account of a particular event. This leads him to record even the sight of a horse urinating. It was this untrained candour which made Seymour so popular with his fox-hunting and sporting clientele, who would have found a more sophisticated approach a dilution of the interesting content of his paintings. Seymour's was, of course, a highly selective realism: only the most important details are prominent. As Seymour scribbled on one of his drawings, 'The best manners is to give the least trouble and not to be too ceremonious.' It was during Seymour's

lifetime, in fact, that sporting art became the concern of a specialized audience. It was viewed with increasing scorn by the rest of the art world and its audience who saw it as uncouth, uncultured and even immoral. It was this stigma which led to the relatively low opinion held of Stubbs's art during his lifetime and to the artist objecting to being described as a 'horse painter'.

TURNER AND THE SOUTH-EAST

Turner's interest in a 'working landscape' is clear in his *Ploughing up Turnips, near Slough* of 1809. The painting has an almost mock-heroic air about it, with its motley group of agricultural labourers and cattle set against a shimmering backdrop dominated by Windsor Castle; the whole is bathed in a subtle light worthy of Claude Lorraine or Aelbert Cuyp. To the right a cow munches some turnips, which are being ploughed up by a worker in the middle of the painting. A bottle and beer mug suggest the hurried refreshment available to the men, while some women to the left take a rest from the heavy work. As in many paintings of this period, the significance of the image lies partly in its specific historical context, which is that of Britain's war against France. Thus the power and beauty of the presence of Windsor Castle, the very image of the state, is seen both to guarantee and be maintained by the labourers' work. Britain's strength, is shown to lie firmly in her landscape.

For much of his career Turner was a frequent

JAMES SEYMOUR
A Kill at Ashdown Park
1743 Oil on canvas
180.3 × 238.8 cm
71 × 94 in

visitor to Petworth in west Sussex, the home of the great patron George Wyndham, third Earl of Egremont. From the late 1820s until Egremont's death in 1837, Turner made a number of his most beautiful paintings at Petworth, four of which were commissioned for the great Grinling Gibbons Carved Room, and whose studies are now in the Tate. Turner also made many drawings, watercolours and gouaches, a fair number showing the artist's fascination not only with Egremont's aesthetic and social culture – his house, landscaped gardens and art collection – but also with his activities as a farmer and business man.

Turner was provided with a special studio at Petworth by the Earl, as the painter George Jones recalled in a manuscript written in 1849 where he describes a trick played on Turner by his friend, the sculptor Sir Francis Chantrey,

When Turner painted a series of
landscapes at Petworth, for the
dining-room, he worked with his

J. M. W. TURNER
Ploughing up Turnips,
near Slough
1809 Oil on canvas
101.9 × 130.2 cm
40⅛ × 51¼ in

THE EARL OF EGREMONT

One of Turner's most important aristocratic patrons was also a great agricultural improver. George Wyndham, 3rd Earl of Egremont, had his seat at Petworth in West Sussex. Here he attracted many artists, who enjoyed the freedom of the fine house and beautiful grounds, generous hospitality and the treasures of a great collection of old master and contemporary British paintings. They also would

Petworth – home in the nineteenth-century of the great patron of the arts, George Wyndham, Earl of Egremont

have been impressed by Egremont's skills and energy as a farmer, entrepreneur and philanthropist, for which he received wide acclaim as a selfless landlord and patriot. Men such as Egremont, who pioneered new agricultural techniques, invested in canal developments and extended their largesse to their workforce, were seen as the vigorous guardians of the country's economic and social strength during the perilous years of the Napoleonic Wars and their aftermath.

door locked against everybody but the master of the house. Chantrey was there at the time, and determined to see what Turner was doing; he imitated Lord Egremont's peculiar step, and the two distinct raps on the door by which his lordship was accustomed to announce himself: and the key being immediately turned, he slipped into the room before the artist could shut him out, which joke was mutually enjoyed by the two attached friends.

One of the greatest of Turner's series of landscapes for the Earl of Egremont is the view of the park with Tillington church in the distance. Like all the Petworth oil paintings, this view has a wide horizontal format which Turner exploited by exaggerating it and creating a kind of wide-angle effect. The resulting distorted perspective, which can be found in a number of Turner's works, has the effect of drawing the viewer into the picture space. To the left the Earl can be seen returning to the house at the end of the day and being greeted by a pack of his dogs who run out towards him in a line.

There is an elegiac feeling to the painting with its wide empty spaces and setting sun, very suitable as an image of a great landowner approaching the end of his life. Indeed, so acute was Turner's vision of Egremont's old age (he was by now in his eighties), that this may be one reason why the painting, which is known to have hung in the Carved Room for a while, was not retained there. As with so many of his most poetic images, Turner has masterfully achieved a poignant sense of the beauty and grandeur of waning power.

THE CHAIN PIER AT BRIGHTON

The Earl of Egremont had financial interests in the building of the Chain Pier at Brighton, which opened in November 1823. One of Turner's paintings for the Carved Room at Petworth was of the Chain Pier and was painted after Constable had exhibited a painting of the same subject at the Royal Academy in 1827.

Unlike Turner, Constable had little interest in modernity and seems to have had scant respect for the urban crowds who increasingly flocked to Brighton for a day by the sea. Constable's reason for visiting Brighton in the 1820s was his wife's ill health and her doctor's advice that she should take some sea air. Constable explained his feelings about the new seaside resort to his

J. M. W. TURNER
Petworth Park: Tillington Church in the Distance
c. 1828 Oil on canvas
60 × 145.7 cm
23⅝ × 57⅜ in

JOHN CONSTABLE
Chain Pier at Brighton
1826-7 Oil on canvas
127 × 182.9 cm
50 × 72 in

friend John Fisher in a letter of August 1824. It gives a remarkable insight into his views on nature, culture and modern society,

> *Brighton is the receptacle of the fashion and off-scouring of London. The magnificence of the sea, and its (to use your own beautifull expression) everlasting voice, is drowned in the din & lost in the tumult of stage coaches – gigs – 'flys' etc. – and the beach is only Piccadilly . . . by the sea-side. Ladies dressed and* undressed *– gentlemen in morning gowns & slippers on, or without them altogether about* knee deep *in the breakers –footmen – children – nursery maids, dogs, boys, fishermen – preventive service men (with hangers and pistols), rotten fish and those hideous amphibious animals the old bathing women, whose language both in oaths & voice resembles men – all are mixed up together in endless & indecent confusion. The genteeler part, the marine parade, is still more unnatural – with its trimmed and neat appearance & the dandy jetty or chain pier, with its long & elegant strides into the sea a full ¼ of a mile. In short there is nothing here for a painter but the breakers – & sky. . . .*

Here is the country Tory's nightmare world: a former fishing village transformed into a fashionable holiday spot where the classes mingle in 'indecent confusion' and the new buildings are 'unnatural' and vulgar. Where Turner, or later William Frith (see page 45), for instance, might have found a lively, if chaotic, human scene, Constable discovers only a frightful image of the consequences of progress and the advancement of social equality.

Constable's painting shows a view from the west looking along the beach to the Chain Pier in the distance and to the left the houses on the sea front. He has deliberately given prominence in the foreground to the fishermen, their boats and tackle, in contrast to the faintly ludicrous bathing huts and crowds of day trippers in the background. Noble work is set off to advantage

ABOVE: *The countryside around Shoreham in Kent was an area that inspired the 'Ancients' and particularly Samuel Palmer to produce such distinctive works as* Coming from Evening Church *1830*

against aimless pleasures. Almost two-thirds of the painting is dominated by a superb cloudy sky, which Constable held to be the 'chief organ of sentiment' in a painting. This truly great painting, exhibited to demolish the claims of more picturesque seaside paintings by artists such as William Collins and Augustus Wall Callcott, failed to sell and remained with Constable until his death ten years later.

SAMUEL PALMER AND THE ANCIENTS

Samuel Palmer's landscape vision shared with Constable's a concern for an established order of things in which each man knew his place within nature and society. In Palmer's case, however, the landscape was a place of spiritual transcendence and the fulfilment of pastoral dreams. After a visit to Dulwich with John Linnell (see page 63) in the early 1820s, Palmer,

who had previously been influenced by David Cox (see page 152), wrote: 'Cox is pretty – is sweet, but not grand, nor profound.... Nature has properties which lie still deeper.' Linnell introduced Palmer to William Blake, the great poet and painter, and the circle of young disciples around him which included the artists Edward Calvert and George Richmond. Palmer described Linnell as a 'good angel from heaven' sent 'to pluck me from the pit of modern art'. Linnell introduced him not only to the work of William Blake but also to 'primitives' from early periods in art such as Pieter Brueghel, Albrecht Dürer and other fifteenth- and sixteenth-century painters.

Palmer first visited the village of Shoreham in God's Heath Hundred, Kent, in the early 1820s, at a time of considerable agricultural unrest; he moved there in 1826 after a bout of ill health. He stayed first at a local farm and then came into possession of a ruinous old cottage which he christened 'Rat Abbey', before finally moving into Water House, off Church Street and on the banks of the River Darenth. This was the house of his father, who had recently been appointed minister of the Baptist chapel at the nearby village of Otford. Water House became the meeting place for a group of young 'exiles' from the town who sought new life in the country and in the exalted study of nature. The 'Ancients', as they called themselves, included Palmer, Calvert, Richmond and other followers of Blake, who were all influenced by the older artist's woodcut illustrations for Virgil's *Eclogues* (1821). Palmer described these tiny, beautifully wrought images as 'visions of little dells, and nooks, and corners of Paradise; models of the

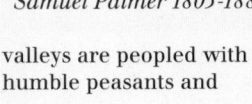

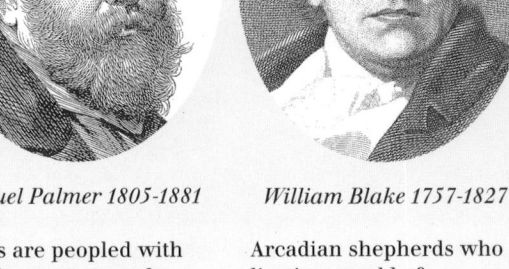

exquisitest pitch of intense poetry'. The Ancients went in search of a landscape around Shoreham which would correspond to Blake's idyllic moonlit vision. Blake, once visited Shoreham to meet his disciples, who took him on a farcical ghost-hunt in Shoreham Place, where Calvert revealed that an extremely eerie noise came from the regular tapping of a snail's shell as it climbed a window.

Coming from Evening Church (1830), a tempera painting on paper mounted on a wood panel, has all the chief characteristics of Palmer's Shoreham landscape art. (Tempera is a medium used in painting and is derived from egg white or yolk mixed with water.) A huge moon casts a rich light over a swelling landscape, in the heart of which lie an ivy-covered church and picturesque cottages. Villagers are shown leaving the church after evensong, holding flowers and apparently moving along in a ritualized trance. This is a Christian landscape where a pagan sense of nature's fecundity, even erotic bounty, recalls the debt to Virgil, whom Palmer believed to have anticipated the coming of Christ in his fourth eclogue. As in the poetry of the classical author, Palmer shows a benevolent nature where even the trees bend to form a primitive Gothic arch. Like many Romantic artists, Palmer looked to the landscape for security and spiritual rejuvenation, as one of his poems reveals,

> With pipe and rural chaunt along,
> The shepherds wind their homeward
>   way,
> And with melodious even song,
> Lull to rest the weary day.
> Low lies their home 'mongst many a
>   hill,
> In fruitful and deep delved womb;
> A little village, safe, and still,
> Where pain and vice full seldom
>   come
> Nor horrid noise of warlike drum.

A technical examination reveals some interesting points about the work which help to explain the rich effects Palmer has achieved. He seems to have drawn with sepia ink on the paper, which had been first coated with white gesso. (Gesso is a white coating of gypsum and glue applied to wood panels to make them suitable for painting on.) This was followed by broad areas of watercolour and then thick impasto for the moon, spire and figures. (Impasto describes paint that has been applied thickly in order to create a textured surface.) Gold powder mixed with size was also mixed into some parts of the surface, and the whole was given a layer of varnish. (Size is a type of glue put on canvas in order to prevent too much paint soaking into it.) On top of this, to create greater unity and quality, Palmer added a thick amber glaze to some areas. Like Blake, Palmer believed such techniques were akin to those of their revered 'primitive' predecessors.

WILLIAM HOLMAN HUNT AND THE PRE-RAPHAELITES

The Ancients were in many respects artistic and spiritual forefathers of the Pre-Raphaelites, who themselves were influenced by Blake as

SAMUEL PALMER
Coming from Evening Church
1830 Tempera on paper
30.2 × 20 cm
11⅞ × 7⅞ in

well as by so-called 'primitive' or early Renaissance art. Much of their work, including their landscapes, was concerned with religious themes; William Holman Hunt's *Our English Coasts, 1852,* for example, had as its subject matter contemporary theological and political issues. Hunt was one of the most committed Pre-Raphaelites both in his concern for 'truth to nature' and his technical procedures.

Hunt's pupil, R. B. Martineau, had parents who lived near Hastings and the town provides the setting for the painting. The precise location depicted is Lovers' Seat, a popular beauty spot overlooking Covehurst Bay. It was here in August 1852 that Hunt took his canvas and, choosing a westward viewpoint, sketched in the main lines of his composition in pencil over a white ground. The details of sheep, flowers and cliffs were painted from different angles and the butterflies in the left foreground studied from a live specimen indoors. Hunt's client for the painting, Charles Maud, insisted on bright

sunny weather in the work, causing the artist considerable difficulties and delaying the completion of the work until late November. The effort was well worth while, as it was the light and colour of the painting which made it such a success. Ruskin went so far as to claim that,

> *It showed us, for the first time in the history of art, the absolutely faithful balances of colour and shade by which actual sunshine may be transposed into a key in which the harmonies possible with material pigments should yet produce the same impressions upon the mind which were caused by the light itself.*

In other words, Ruskin saw the work as one of the highest achievements of naturalism in art, the creation of a likeness of nature.

The painting's meaning to a contemporary audience, however, did not lie only in its immaculate craftsmanship and powerful colour. At a time when there were fears of invasion by

WILLIAM HOLMAN HUNT
Our English Coasts, 1852 (Strayed Sheep)
1852 Oil on canvas
43.2 × 58.4 cm
17 × 23 in

WILLIAM HOLMAN HUNT

A fascinating exhibition mounted by the Tate's Conservation Department in 1982 showed that the artist William Holman Hunt's immense success as a naturalist in art was largely due to his technical skill and experimentation. Hunt was well versed in the literature of painting materials and techniques and was in correspondence with the leading chemists of the day. The discovery of new compounds by such men led in the nineteenth century to the creation of pigments which allowed completely new effects to be achieved. Among these were chrome red and yellow, cadmium yellow, cobalt green, yellow and blue, ultramarine violets and various 'alizarins'. ('Alizarins' are pigments made from a coal tar

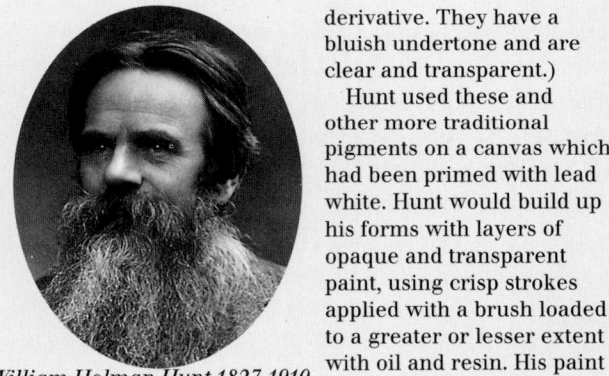

William Holman Hunt 1827-1910

derivative. They have a bluish undertone and are clear and transparent.)

Hunt used these and other more traditional pigments on a canvas which had been primed with lead white. Hunt would build up his forms with layers of opaque and transparent paint, using crisp strokes applied with a brush loaded to a greater or lesser extent with oil and resin. His paint was creamy in consistency and dried to a hard, enamel-like surface. Examined closely his technique creates an almost hallucinatory effect. This has a particularly strong impact where Hunt uses brilliant greens in the sunlit areas and purples and blues in the shadows. The notion of coloured shadows was later a key feature of Impressionist painting.

France, the sheep, wandering close to danger and entangled in the undergrowth, were interpreted as a satirical image of Britain's inadequate coastal defences. The painting was also entitled *Strayed Sheep* by Hunt when it was exhibited, ironically, in Paris in 1855. This suggests its religious symbolism and comments on the flock losing its way as a result of wranglings over doctrine within the Church of England.

WILLIAM POWELL FRITH AND GEORGE PRICE BOYCE

Two paintings of almost the same date form an intriguing pair in connection with Victorian attitudes to nature and to society. These are George Price Boyce's *Girl by a Beech Tree in a Landscape* (1857) and William Powell Frith's *Derby Day* (1856-8).

Frith's painting is, of course, one of the most

famous Victorian paintings of all time and caused a sensation when it was exhibited at the Royal Academy in 1858. It shows a crowd at Epsom on one of the great popular days in the racing calendar. All classes of society can be seen here, from the wealthy ladies and gentlemen waiting for the contents of their lavish hamper to be laid out for them, to the old fortune-teller and the urchins hoping to pick up some scraps. Frith is interested in particular facial types and in individual behaviour. A self-satisfied dandy in a top hat to the right trifles with a poor flower girl, while his shamefaced mistress sits awkwardly in her carriage. An acrobat's accomplice is momentarily distracted by the sight of the fresh lobster and game pies being arranged by the footman, while under a carriage a rather brutish boy reaches out for an empty bottle in the hope of a few dregs. To the left of the painting, near a gaming tent, a

WILLIAM POWELL FRITH
Derby Day
1856-8 Oil on canvas
101.6 × 223.5 cm
40 × 88 in

GEORGE PRICE BOYCE
Girl by a Beech Tree in a Landscape
1857 Oil on board
29.8 × 47.9 cm
11¾ × 18⅞ in
Boyce uses almost invisibly fine strokes to depict the fine details of the grass, foliage and surface of the huge old beech in the foreground.

country lad in his smock is restrained from losing his money by his wary girlfriend, while nearby a smartly dressed office boy discovers he has been fleeced by the men playing the three-thimble trick. In the background Frith shows the grandstands, horses, jockeys and milling crowds, studies for which were made from photographs he had already taken. Following Pre-Raphaelite principles, Frith carefully depicts every detail of the scene with meticulous precision.

The great attraction of the painting for Frith's contemporaries lay in its variety of social types, narrative content and high naturalism. The Victorian audience was fascinated by such images of their class-ridden and complex society and enjoyed the opportunity to subject the details to painstaking analysis and to draw conclusions from them. In this case the great amusement offered by the human drama would have been tempered by anxiety about the prevalence of drinking, gambling, sexual impropriety and the alarming gulf that existed between rich and poor. Although the race course at Epsom was in the countryside, its invasion every year by crowds of avid race-goers was a reminder of the fragile beauty of the landscape and the immense problems caused by urbanization. Like Constable, Ruskin was critical of the city's culture and looked to the natural world for moral standards by which men and women might gauge their physical and spiritual condition and conduct. In writing about a landscape painting by George Boyce in his *Academy Notes* in 1858 he judged it to be: 'Full of truth and sweet feeling. How pleasant it is, after looking long at Frith's picture, to see how happy a little girl may be who hasn't gone to the Derby!' It is possible, from the evidence available, that the work he was referring to is Boyce's *Girl by a Beech Tree in a Landscape,* the only signed oil painting by the artist. Boyce was a close friend of many of the Pre-Raphaelite painters and was best known for his watercolour landscape and architectural paintings. The Tate oil painting by him is a classic example of the intense naturalism advocated in the 1850s by his mentor Ruskin, for whom the figure of the girl in the sunlit landscape was the very image of innocence, truth and natural beauty.

WILLIAM DYCE

Shortly after this Academy summer exhibition, William Dyce began working on *Pegwell Bay, Kent – A Recollection of October 5th 1858* and exhibited it in 1860. Dyce, a Scottish painter, had studied in Rome where he came under the influence of the German Nazarene artists, a devout group whose ideas and style influenced the Pre-Raphaelites. Dyce, a favourite of Prince Albert, had many varied intellectual and scientific interests; he was also an arts administrator, and decorated the new Houses of Parliament with frescoes. He was a devout High Anglican, an authority on church ritual, music and doctrine, and he painted many religious works. It was Dyce who persuaded Ruskin to look at the work of the young emerging Pre-Raphaelite artists in 1850.

His painting of Pegwell Bay is in fact an image of religious doubt in an age of scientific discovery. Where Boyce showed nature as an unproblematic source of truth and beauty, Dyce presents an ominous scene of isolated figures threatened by vast, mind-numbing forces. Dyce stayed at Pegwell Bay, near Ramsgate, in the autumn of 1858 and is probably the figure on the extreme right who is carrying artist's equipment and looking up at the comet shooting across the sky. The figures in the foreground are Dyce's wife, his two sisters-in-law and one of his sons. Two of the women are collecting seashells and fossils while the tide is out, and the boy and his mother look out of the picture to their right. The figures seem alienated from one another and the feeling is one of time having stopped. The critic D. S. MacColl, writing in 1902, thought it was 'as if the man had come to the ugly end of the world and felt bound to tell'. The 'recollection' of the title is that of the comet first observed by the astronomer G. B. Donati on 2 June 1858, which was at its most brilliant on the date to which Dyce refers.

WILLIAM DYCE
Pegwell Bay, Kent – A Recollection of October 5th 1858
1859-60 Oil on canvas
63.5 × 88.9 cm
25 × 35 in

GEORGE CLAUSEN
Winter Work
1883-4 Oil on canvas
77.5 × 92.1 cm
30½ × 36¼ in
Clausen's rough-textured image of dreary rural toil is given a sentimental touch by the sad look the woman on the right gives the young girl. The latter stands with her hoop watching her future existence where play will be so limited.

Traditionally comets have been seen as bad omens, but here Dyce's interest seems to be more in the impact of Tennyson's 'terrible muses', geology and astronomy, on man's religious faith. The comet and the cliffs represent the vast, unknowable realms of space and time which science was opening up and which were leaving man in a position of doubt and insecurity. The great Victorian geologist Charles Lyell had written that, 'the geologist may admire the ample limits of his domain, and admit, at the same time, that not only the exterior of the planet but the entire earth, is but an atom in the midst of the countless worlds surveyed by the astronomer.' This sense of distance and complexity is the subject of Dyce's work and echoes Matthew Arnold's frightening poem 'Dover Beach', with its 'grating roar of pebbles' and 'eternal note of sadness' in a world on the brink of faithlessness.

GEORGE CLAUSEN

Such metaphysical anxiety was less bothersome to painters in the late nineteenth century than concern about man's social existence.

George Clausen's *Winter Work* (1883-4) was painted at Childwick Green, near St Albans, where the artist settled with his wife in 1881, having lived in Hampstead before this. His explanation for the move is typical of those young 'rustic naturalists' who looked to the agricultural conditions of the time for the subject matter,

We went because it was cheaper to live, and there were better opportunities of working. One saw people doing simple things under good conditions of lighting; and there was always landscape. And nothing was made easy for you: you had to dig out what you wanted.

During this period Clausen also had two spells in Paris and Brittany, perfecting the style he had developed from the example of the French naturalist painter, Jules Bastien-Lepage. Clausen supported Bastien-Lepage during a dispute over the latter's artistic merit which occurred in London in 1880 when *Les Foins*, his large painting of two exhausted field workers, was exhibited. Pre-Raphaelites, Symbolists and others were critical of the Frenchman's rather dour, tonal *plein-air* (open-air) style, even though he had gathered around him many young disciples such as Clausen.

Winter Work shows labourers topping and tailing beet for sheep fodder and was the result of many drawings, notes and photographic studies. Few critics liked the work with its grim colour, rough texture and unprepossessing figures. This is the very antithesis of Samuel Palmer's Arcadian landscape vision. In Clausen's world there is no protective valley or glow of moonbeams, only cold earth and the certainty of grinding, repetitive work. Clausen uses a high horizon to emphasize further the workers' oppressed condition.

CHARLES CONDER

Charles Conder's charming work *Windy Day at Brighton* was painted at the beginning of this century in a loosely Impressionist style. A few figures are shown walking along the promenade, while in the central foreground a young girl flies a kite above a group of women turning the corner. In front of them a bowler-hatted

man, reputed to be the painter Walter Sickert, walks past a doorway. The painting is rather typical of the anecdotal Impressionism prevalent in the circle of artists known as the New English Art Club.

Conder is best known for his Arcadian fantasies, fan designs and other decorative work and this is evident in the light, almost rococo touch in his painting. He had studied in Paris in the 1890s and been influenced not only by contemporaries such as Claude Monet, Louis Anquetin, James Abbott McNeill Whistler and Pierre Puvis de Chavannes but also by the work of eighteenth-century painters such as Jean Antoine Watteau and by Japanese art. In these interests Conder, the inveterate aesthete and fantasist, reveals himself to have been in many respects a typical *fin-de-siècle* artist.

SPENCER GORE

A reaction to the ethos of the 'naughty nineties', of which Conder was a classic representative, can be discerned in the work of the artists of the

CHARLES CONDER
Windy Day at Brighton
c. 1904-5 Oil on canvas
63.5 × 91.4 cm
25 × 36 in

Camden Town Group. (These artists are dealt with in greater detail on pages 71–73.) One of their number, Spencer Gore, lived for some months in 1912 in Letchworth, Hertfordshire, at the home of the painter Harold Gilman. Letchworth was a new garden city and must have been for Gore a complete contrast to the run-down parts of north London that he had previously painted. *The Cinder Path,* which is devoid of narrative interest, shows a path that ran from the end of Works Road in Letchworth across the field to Baldock. The paint is applied drily using strong contrasts of mauve and green. The forms are described with angular, broken lines which stress the geometrical aspects of the scene. This emphasis on flat patterning and structure is a notable feature of Camden Town painting after 1912 and shows the influence of Gauguin, Cézanne and even the Cubist art of Picasso and Braque. Like many painters at this time, Gore was struggling with the need to give his art a 'constructive' quality without sacrificing a strong impulse to record the appearance of things. 'It has always been the objective of the great imaginative painters', he wrote, 'to reconcile their ideas with the things they saw.' Gore died of pneumonia in March 1914, which was considered by many artists to be a great loss to British painting.

STANLEY SPENCER

Like Gore, Stanley Spencer studied at the Slade School of Art but, although he shared a similar

SPENCER GORE
The Cinder Path
1912 Oil on canvas
68.6 × 78.7 cm
27 × 31 in

training with the older artist, his world view was utterly different. *Swan Upping at Cookham,* begun in 1914 and finished after the artist's demobilization in 1919, shows Spencer's offbeat imaginative vision of his birthplace in Berkshire. Spencer wrote that 'places in Cookham seem to be possessed of a sacred presence of which the inhabitants are not aware.'

In his painting the theme taken is the annual 'swan upping', when officials of the Companies of Vintners and Dyers, who by royal licence own the swans on the Thames, gather the young swans for marking. Spencer shows the birds being taken ashore in a carpenter's bags at the landing stage near the bridge at Ferry Hotel in Cookham. Spencer recalled that the idea for the image came to him in church: 'I could hear the people going to the river as I sat in our north aisle pew,' he wrote, and said this provoked him to take the 'in-church feeling out of church' and transfer it to the nearby Thames. Spencer did not make studies of the river setting because he wanted his spiritual vision to remain untainted by external influences.

Spencer is well known for his religious images such as *The Resurrection, Cookham* and is usually seen as part of the British tradition of eccentric visionary artists which includes William Blake, Samuel Palmer and Eric Gill. His precise religious views are not altogether clear and may reflect the split in his family between his father, who attended Church of England services, and his mother, who took Spencer to the Nonconformist chapel. He even dallied at one point,

LEFT: The bridge over the Thames at Cookham in Berkshire – scene of the annual 'Swan Upping'

STANLEY SPENCER
Swan Upping at Cookham
1914-19 Oil on canvas
148 × 116.2 cm
58¼ × 45¾ in

PAUL NASH AND THE
INFLUENCE OF GIORGIO DE CHIRICO

In the late 1920s Paul Nash's work was considerably influenced by the paintings of the Italian artist Giorgio de Chirico. The latter had been very important in the development of Surrealism, which in turn had helped to change the course of Nash's career after about 1925. De Chirico's work of the period 1910-20 had used distorted perspective, simple geometrical forms, strong shadows and incongruous combinations of objects to create disquieting dreamscapes. Nash used these devices to evolve a unique vision based on the

Paul Nash 1889-1946

British landscape. His art is distinguished by dry, pastel shades and a firm pictorial structure. Nash was an enthusiastic reader of old

manuals on perspective and also of the works of the seventeenth-century physician and antiquarian, Sir Thomas Browne. In the early 1930s he made designs for *Urne Buriall and the Garden of Cyrus* by Browne who had stressed 'how nature Geometrizeth, and observeth order in all things'. The orchard at Nash's home at Iden, with its regularly spaced trees and straight fences, is a flawed image of the divinely ordered garden based on Browne's 'mystical Mathematicks of the City of Heaven'.

PAUL NASH
Landscape at Iden
1929 Oil on canvas
69.8 × 90.8 cm
27½ × 35¾ in

ERIC RAVILIOUS
The Vale of the White Horse
c. 1939 Watercolour
45.1 × 32.4 cm
17¾ × 12¾ in

under the influence of Eric Gill, with Roman Catholicism. Whatever his exact doctrinal inclinations may have been, Spencer's religiosity and search for the spiritual in everyday life are indisputable. He wrote in 1944,

> *Somehow religion was something to do with me, and I was to do with religion. It came into my vision quite naturally, like the sky and rain. . . . I am still faithfully trying to turn and keep in the Christian direction.*

PAUL NASH

Paul Nash's *Landscape at Iden* (1929) shows the view from the back garden at Oxenbridge Cottage, Iden, near Rye in Sussex, where he had been living since 1925. Previously the artist had lived nearby at Dymchurch on the coast.

The countryside around Iden, with its rich agricultural land, was very different from his former home, as can be seen in Nash's view looking through an orchard, across the Rother Valley to the Isle of Oxney. Nash's interests, however, are not those of a Constable or Clausen, who would have shown men or women at work in such a landscape. Nash's scene is empty of human presence, perhaps rather ominously so. In the stage-like foreground a solitary upright stake and a log-basket are flanked by the sharply receding forms of a wattle fence and a tall screen which draw the eye to a large truncated pyramid of logs and, on the far side of the orchard, a white gate.

A snake wraps itself around one of the lintels of the fence to the left of the logpile. Simplified hills and clouds in a grey-blue sky suggest escape from the faintly threatening enclosure of the orchard and foreground area. The possibility of danger or evil is implied by the snake.

ERIC RAVILIOUS

One of Paul Nash's students at the Royal College of Art in the 1920s was Eric Ravilious, who is best known for his wood engravings, textile designs and watercolours. Ravilious had a similar feeling to Nash for the British landscape and its mysterious history, although whatever elements of surrealism and abstract art can be found in his work are far less obvious than in that of his teacher. Nevertheless, like Nash's, his landscape has both a powerful structure and a sense of drama and revelation.

In the late 1930s he made a series of watercolours of the chalk figures cut in the downs of southern England. One of these was of the White Horse on White Horse Hill, Berkshire, which is probably an Iron Age tribal emblem. Ravilious's skills with watercolour were perfect for capturing the chalky soils and undulating shapes of the Berkshire Downs. The horse itself

GRAHAM BELL
Dover Front
1938 Oil on canvas
63.5 × 76.2 cm
25 × 30 in

lies on the most distant hill under a cold but radiant grey sky. As with most of Ravilious's landscape paintings, however, there is an illusory quality which works in counterpoint to the sense of being in front of a strikingly real view. This stems in part from the clarity of his design and the cleanness of execution. Parts seem to intersect one another crisply and in this respect Ravilious's art has some affinities with the work of eighteenth- and early nineteenth-century watercolourists such as Francis Towne and John Sell Cotman. Like their work Ravilious's is pleasurable not only for its evocative imagery but also for its physical quality as watercolour and pencil on paper. Ravilious went missing on 2 September 1942 on a flight near Iceland while on duty as a war artist.

THE EUSTON ROAD SCHOOL

Ravilious was friendly with the artists who formed the Euston Road School in the late 1930s. They were dedicated, in an age dominated by surrealism and constructivism, to a realist art which often dealt with social and political issues. Their work should be seen in the context of the general sympathy among artists and intellectuals of the time with left-wing political causes and it has strong affinities with the documentary films of John Grierson and the investigations of Mass Observation, the organization of volunteer social observers started before the Second World War. Indeed it was while working with Grierson that one of the leading figures in the Euston Road School, William Coldstream, decided that modern art had become too introverted and esoteric. In many respects, Coldstream, Graham Bell and their associates continued the tradition of the Camden Town Group of the pre-1914 period.

Graham Bell, who was born in South Africa and came to England in 1931, was one of the most talented artists of the Euston Road School. He was also one of the most politically radical members of the group and in a pamphlet published in 1939, called 'The Artist and his Public', asserted that the poor relationship between the two was,

the inevitable result of capitalism. . . . The rich have grown to hate art (as they hate all serious things) because it reminds them of their guilt. They have communicated their dislike to the in-between classes and to the poor by way of a doctored press and a narcotic cinema. This isolation from patronage and popularity forces artists towards a self-destructive obscurity.

Bell's solution was a social transformation along Marxist lines. As an artist he hoped to contribute to this change by painting, in an accessible though disciplined style, images of contemporary reality and significance.

His view of *Dover Front* was painted in June and July 1938 while he was in the town on a commission, incongruously enough, to paint the 'white cliffs' for the International Business Machines Corporation. The figure in the hat and overcoat to the right of the picture is Anne Olivier Popham, who later remembered that Bell 'sat . . . on the windowsill in a small railed-in area at the side of one of the tall stuccoed and canopied houses to the southern end of the front'. The painting is characterized by a light brush stroke which creates a delicate and rational pictorial structure. The art historian Kenneth Clark described Bell as aiming at 'the science of Cézanne to express the vision of Corot', and certainly the artist was heavily indebted to his study of these two great French landscape painters. There is a fastidious geometrical quality in Bell's work which derives mainly from his study of Paul Cézanne's painting. It is interesting to note that Sir Anthony Blunt, the art historian who later was discovered to have been a communist spy, saw in such works as this by Bell an antidote to what he saw as the decadence of the kind of art typified by Picasso's famous *Guernica* – a 'distorted' modern painting which the artist considered expressed his horror at the fascist bombing of a small Spanish town in 1937. For Bell, Blunt and their associates the style of Picasso's *Guernica* and other similar art was only accessible to a tiny minority, not to the great mass of people.

LONDON

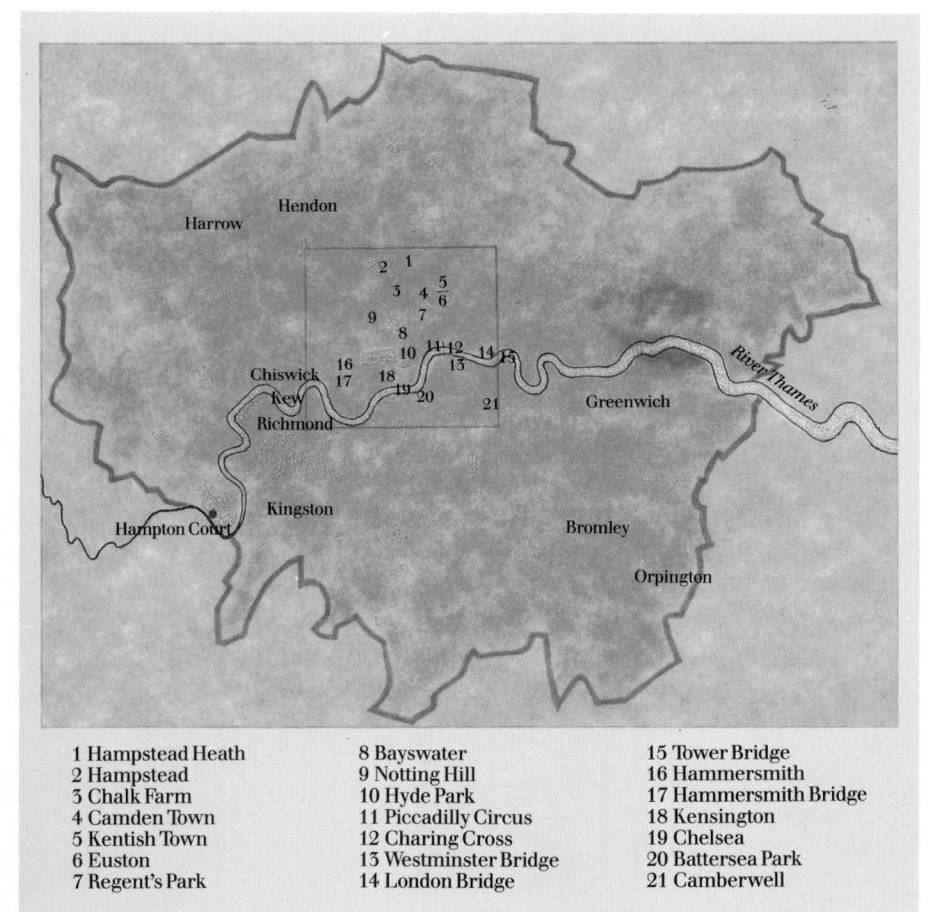

1 Hampstead Heath	8 Bayswater	15 Tower Bridge
2 Hampstead	9 Notting Hill	16 Hammersmith
3 Chalk Farm	10 Hyde Park	17 Hammersmith Bridge
4 Camden Town	11 Piccadilly Circus	18 Kensington
5 Kentish Town	12 Charing Cross	19 Chelsea
6 Euston	13 Westminster Bridge	20 Battersea Park
7 Regent's Park	14 London Bridge	21 Camberwell

LEFT: London with all its cosmopolitan variety, has presented artists with an infinite range of views and subjects over the centuries

The city of London, with its tremendous scale and variety, presents an almost infinite range of views and subjects for the artist to choose from. Even at the height of the Romantic 'return to nature' it was possible to paint the villages of Chelsea and Kensington, which were then on London's outskirts, and evoke a rural world far away from the crowded, smoky slumland which horrified writers such as Thomas Carlyle and Charles Booth in the nineteenth century.

The Thames has been a persistent and powerful attraction for artists since the seventeenth century. The Italian artist Giovanni Antonio Canaletto painted it as a sparkling route through a spotless city in the eighteenth century, while the American J.A.M. Whistler made it a modern counterpart to Canaletto's native Venice over a

today will be the unlikely subjects of great London landscapes in the future.

BALTHAZAR NEBOT

Balthazar Nebot's *Covent Garden Market* (1737) shows the famous piazza from the south-east, with St Paul's church and the sundial column to the left, and the arcade of the north side on the right. In the foreground, on the south side of the piazza, are fruit and vegetable stalls, the nucleus of the market, which grew rapidly from about the date of this painting.

Nebot, a painter of Spanish descent who worked in Covent Garden, specialized in such open-air views and painted a series of market scenes in the 1730s. His interest lay not only in the topography of the city but also in its human

BALTHAZAR NEBOT
Covent Garden Market
1737 Oil on canvas
63.5 × 123.2 cm
25 × 48½ in

hundred years later. For the artist George Vicat Cole it presented an opportunity to convey the turbulent prowess of the heart of a powerful empire.

While many artists have painted the obvious great buildings, panoramic views and tourist spots, others have looked at the underside of London which cannot be found in the official guide books. They have constantly found unexpected beauty and visual excitement in areas that are either 'off the map' or so obvious that their poetry goes unnoticed. It may well be that the places shunned by Londoners and visitors

meanings. His art combines a Canaletto-like concern for buildings and light effects, with a Hogarthian fascination for the people who live, work and play in the expanding urban world. William Hogarth, who became one of the most successful of Nebot's contemporaries, had only a few years earlier produced the *Harlot's Progress* and *Rake's Progress*, narratives which satirized London life and warned of the dangers of the city for the young and naïve. Nebot, although showing very little moral or novelesque tendency, presents a complex social world centred on trade.

SAMUEL SCOTT

Samuel Scott, who was born in Covent Garden around 1702, specialized at first in sea-pieces, including dramatic views of naval battles. However, after Canaletto's great success with London views in his first year in England (1746), Scott began to paint similar images. One fine example is *An Arch of Westminster Bridge,* painted around 1750. 'Old' Westminster Bridge was built by the Swiss-born engineer Charles Labelye between 1739 and 1750. It was the second bridge to be built across the Thames in London and was eventually demolished in the 1850s to make way for the present Westminster Bridge. It became a popular subject for topographical artists.

Scott made many sketches of the bridge during the course of its construction, and these served as the basis for a number of paintings. The studies were made from a landing-stage to the west of the bridge. The painting shown here depicts the second and third arches of Labelye's magnificent Portland and Purbeck stone construction and allows a view of the north bank of the Thames towards the City. From left to right the buildings include the Fishmarket Wharf, Montagu House, various grand private houses, the wooden York Buildings Water Tower and, through the right-hand arch, the Savoy hotel, St Mary-le-Strand and old Somerset House. Different-sized boats are shown working the river or docked at wharves, while in the foreground to the right two men can be seen swimming. Scott's painting focuses in particular on the completion of one of the domed turrets on the piers of the bridge. Two masons on a wooden platform appear to be celebrating their achievement by sharing a jug of beer. Behind them, to the left, people's heads can be seen between the balusters which run along the top of

SAMUEL SCOTT
An Arch of Westminster Bridge
c. 1750 Oil on canvas
135.3 × 163.8 cm
53¼ × 64½ in

the bridge. There is an understated but nevertheless strong sense of occasion and importance about the painting, entirely fitting for a feat of engineering which symbolized London's extraordinary expansion and development in the eighteenth century.

THOMAS GIRTIN AND J. M. W. TURNER

The tragically short-lived Thomas Girtin was considered by many of his contemporaries to be an even greater painter than his friend J. M. W. Turner. Certainly the beautiful *White House at*

THOMAS GIRTIN
White House at Chelsea
1800 Watercolour
29.8 × 51.4 cm
11¾ × 20¼ in
The wide expanse of water at sunset shown here by Girtin resembles the artist's views for his Eidometropolis, *or* Panorama of London, *shown at Spring Gardens in August 1802, and now lost. In this view however the effect is of rural tranquility whereas the Panorama emphasised the scale and complexity of London with its busy river and multitude of buildings.*

Chelsea (1800) shows Girtin to have been an artist of considerable and daring talent. The house is shown as the source of brilliant sunset reflections on a stretch of the Thames. The painting was apparently held in awe by Turner, as a famous anecdote reveals,

A dealer went one day to Turner, and, after looking round all his drawings in the room, had the audacity to say, 'I have a drawing out there, in my hackney coach, finer than any of yours.' Turner bit his lip,

looked first angry, then meditative.
At length he broke silence: 'Then I tell
you what it is. You have got Tom
Girtin's White House at Chelsea.'
Interestingly enough, two of Turner's late Swiss sketches bear inscriptions by the artist naming 'White House' and 'Girtin', as if Turner himself felt they rivalled Thomas Girtin's work.

Girtin's tranquil view, with its tree-lined horizon, windmill, dominant sky, deep expanse of water and elegant boats, shows London in a pastoral, untroubled mood. Nine years later Turner exhibited, at his own gallery in Queen Anne Street West, an entirely different view of the metropolis seen from Greenwich, a vantage-point popular with a great number of artists. The high viewpoint gives a wide panorama of the city, which Turner presents in all its smog-filled modernity. The verses from his own hand, which he chose to complement the painting, give a clear sense of the image he wished to convey,

Where burthen's Thames reflects the
crowded sail,
Commercial care and busy toil
prevail,
Whose murky veil, aspiring to the
skies,
Obscures thy beauty, and thy form
denies,
Save whereby thy spires pierce the
doubtful air,
As gleams of hope amidst a world of
care.

Turner's fascination with industrialization is well known, as are his reservations about its effects; these are made clear in his poetry. In this painting there is a sense that the countryside is losing ground to the monstrous growth of the city and that the deer and humans enjoying themselves in the foreground have only a fragile and transitory freedom. In the city itself, the spires of London's great eighteenth-century

J. M. W. TURNER
London
1809 Oil on canvas
90.2 × 120 cm
35½ × 47¼ in

churches come under threat from the factory chimneys with their belching choking smoke which 'aspires' to the skies. Turner's art frequently contrasted opposites, creating an uncertain and energetic subject.

JOHN LINNELL

John Linnell and William Mulready frequently painted in the Bayswater and Notting Hill areas of west London where the latter lived from 1809. Kensington Gravel Pits was a small rural village at what is now the junction of Notting Hill Gate and Kensington Church Street; the gravel pits themselves were just to the south of the junction by Kensington Gardens. When Linnell painted his view of men at work in the gravel pits he was lodging at a house on the Edgware Road. He attended evening life classes with Mulready at the Royal Academy during this period and this is evident in the muscular figures, who are derived from Renaissance prototypes. A Michelangelesque pose appears three times, in fact. Linnell employs strong contrasts of light and shade which heighten the impact of the detail in the picture. The impulse towards this kind of

plein-air (open-air) high-focus naturalism came in part from Linnell's conversion to Baptism in 1811 and his reading of William Paley's *Natural Theology*. This book, among other influences, led him to believe that the landscape and its minutely complex organization, as perceived by the analytical eye, were proof of God's presence in all things.

As with the Pre-Raphaelites and their supporter John Ruskin forty years later, the notion of 'truth to nature' in art was identified with a powerful spiritual faith. It was this Nonconformist Protestant vision which led to Linnell's later becoming a disciple of William Blake and eventually, a little ironically, to a far less scientific attitude which produced rather dreamy, if intense, pastoral scenes.

JOHN CONSTABLE IN LONDON

John Constable had little interest in the new industrialized world. His London landscapes are predominantly views of Hampstead Heath, where he lived with his family for long periods from 1819 because of his wife's poor health. It was at Hampstead in 1819 and the early 1820s

JOHN LINNELL
Kensington Gravel Pits
1811-12 Oil on canvas
71.1 × 106.7 cm
28 × 42 in

JOHN CONSTABLE
*Hampstead Heath with
a Rainbow*
1836 Oil on canvas
50.8 × 76.2 cm
20 × 30 in

*BELOW: Hampstead Heath,
where John Constable and
his family lived for long
periods from 1819 till the
artist's death in 1837*

that Constable began his 'skying' – studies, usually in oil or crayon, of different clouds and skies, in which he often noted the time, wind direction and other meteorological details. On one, for instance, he wrote '5th of September, 1822. 10 o'clock, morning, looking south-east, brisk wind at west. Very bright and fresh grey clouds running fast over a yellow bed, about half-way in the sky.'

Constable believed too many lanscapes evaded the importance of the sky, the 'chief organ of sentiment', and were often only a 'white sheet' behind the main scenery. 'The sky is the "source of light" in nature – and governs every thing,' he wrote, although warning against skies becoming too dominant. 'Their difficulty in painting both as to composition and execution is very great, because with all their brilliancy and consequence, they ought not to come forward or be hardly thought about in a picture. . . .'

One of Constable's last landscapes is *Hampstead Heath with a Rainbow*, painted in 1836, the year before his death, for his friend the amateur artist W. George Jennings. Like many of his Hampstead scenes, this shows the view

over Branch Hill Pond; a bank rising steeply on the right partially obscures the view. In the distance lie the fields around Harrow, Hendon and Kilburn. The windmill here is an invention which may have been a nostalgic evocation of the aged painter's native Suffolk. Constable was particularly proud of this canvas, as he told George Constable of Arundel,

> I have lately turned out one of my best bits of Heath, so fresh, so bright, dewy & sunshiny, that I preferred to any former effort, at about 2 feet 6, painted for a very old friend – an amateur who well knows how to appreciate it, for I now see that I shall never be able to paint down to ignorance. Almost all the world is ignorant and vulgar.

tremely popular and evoked proud feelings in British viewers. In this case pride was further bolstered by association with a great military victory. John Rennie's bridge was opened by the Prince Regent on 18 June 1817, the second anniversary of the Battle of Waterloo, amidst great popular festivity. Constable shows the prince embarking at Whitehall Stairs to make the short journey up the river to the new bridge. On the right the Lord Mayor's magnificent barge can be seen. Beyond the north end of the bridge is Somerset House, the home of the Royal Academy at the time, while at the other end stands the Shot Tower. This latter architectural detail is anomalous, as it was not built until 1826, some nine years after the event recorded by Constable.

Although Constable probably witnessed the

JOHN CONSTABLE
The Opening of Waterloo Bridge
1832 Oil on canvas
134.6 × 219.7 cm
53 × 86½ in

As ever, Constable places his art in opposition to what he saw as the degraded condition of the modern world.

An unusual and spectacular painting of London by Constable is *The Opening of Waterloo Bridge* (1832), which commemorates an event which took place fifteen years earlier. It is not clear why he painted this image nor why he persisted with it for so long. It is hardly a typical Constable scene and he seems to have found it inordinately difficult to complete. In 1824, in fact, he confessed to a friend that 'I am impressed with an idea that it will ruin me.'

Of course, as we have seen with Scott's painting of Westminster Bridge some eighty years before, views of London bridges were ex-

opening of the bridge in 1817, he does not apear to have made any drawings of it until 1819. From that year on there are numerous references to the work in Constable's diaries, which show him at one moment despairing of the project, the next taking it up again with renewed enthusiasm. Characteristically, the year he exhibited it, Constable told the engraver David Lucas, 'I am dashing away at the great London – and why not? I may as well produce this abortion as another – for who cares for landscape?' The surface of Constable's troubled masterpiece is in fact heavily worked and has almost the look of some jewelled and gilded ornament. It bears all the signs of the great effort it entailed, although it certainly impressed Turner

FORD MADOX BROWN

Ford Madox Brown was both a forerunner and an associate of the Pre-Raphaelite artists. He is best known for his religious, historical and contemporary 'social-issue' paintings, but often turned to landscape in-between his major works.

Born in Calais, Brown trained in Belgium, and studied in Paris and Rome where he was influenced by the German 'Nazarene' painters and by Italian Renaissance art. He also visited Basle where he was much impressed by the

Ford Madox Brown 1821-93

work of Holbein. In 1848 the young D. G. Rossetti applied

to have lessons with him in London where he had settled. They became very good friends and Brown gave great encouragement to Rossetti and the Pre-Raphaelites with whose aims in art he was in great sympathy. In the 1860s Brown designed furniture and stained glass for William Morris and during the last fifteen years of his life worked on an extremely ambitious mural scheme in Manchester Town Hall.
He died in 1893.

FORD MADOX BROWN
The Hayfield
1855-6 Oil on panel
24.1 × 33.3 cm
9½ × 13⅛ in

who, it is said, upon seeing it on the Academy walls a few days before the exhibition opened, added a large dab of red to one of his own works which hung nearby.

FORD MADOX BROWN

When Ford Madox Brown painted *The Hayfield* in 1855-6, Hendon was an agricultural area known for its hay-farming. Today, of course, it is part of the sprawling suburbs of north London,

much of it built between the wars; within its boundaries run major roads and motorways. Brown's view shows the Tenterden estate looking east towards a house which catches the setting sun on its west face. The artist is shown in the foreground surrounded by his painting equipment and taking a rest. To the right a farm worker on horseback oversees the last work of the day, while some children take a ride on the back of a haycart. Such carts made a daily journey to Cumberland Market, near Regent's

J. A. M. WHISTLER
*Nocturne in Blue and
Gold: Old Battersea
Bridge*
c. 1872-5 Oil on canvas
67.9 × 50.8 cm
26¾ × 20 in
*Whistler would brush
heavily diluted runny paint
over a canvas primed with
grey and red. He frequently
allowed a single colour, in
this case blue, to dominate
a work to create a
musically expressive mood.*

one made at Cumberland Market and the figure of himself from a 'lay figure' arranged in his conservatory. By 27 January 1856, having retouched much of the landscape section and having now spent a hundred hours on it, he was still dissatisfied with the painting. There are certainly problems in the foreground where the light is inexactly achieved and the surface is a little uncertain. This is not the case, however, with the brilliant background where Brown has perfectly realized the superb colours he described as being the result of the weather the year he painted the scene:

> The stacking of the second crop of
> hay had been much delayed by rain,
> which heightened the green of the
> remaining grass, together with the
> brown of the hay. The consequence
> was an effect of unusual beauty of
> colour, making the hay by contrast
> with the green grass, positively red
> or pink, under the glow of twilight
> here represented.

Somewhat ironically it was this intense colour which his dealer objected to in the painting; it resulted in the picture's purchase by the great designer William Morris when he was still a young disciple of Brown's Pre-Rapahelite friend, Dante Gabriel Rossetti.

JAMES ABBOT MCNEILL WHISTLER

The great adversary of the Pre-Raphaelite philosophy of 'truth to nature' and in particular of its most powerful critical exponent, John Ruskin, was the American painter and eccentric dandy, James Abbot McNeill Whistler. Whistler had come under the influence of the French realist painter, Gustave Courbet, in the 1850s and then switched allegiance to the Impressionists. He was particularly impressed with Japanese art, when it became fashionable with avant-garde artists such as Edouard Manet and Edgar Degas in Paris in the 1860s. Whistler, who had spent a number of years in the French capital, moved to London in 1859, where he settled in Chelsea by the river.

Whistler incorporated many features of both Impressionist and oriental art into his work. The former stimulated his interest in particular light effects and a loosened brushwork, while from the latter he learned the subtle art of asymmetrical composition and the use of unconventional viewpoints. The result of these influences was an art which suppressed detail in favour of a frequently misty atmosphere and

Park, during the harvest season.

On 21 July 1855, having spent some time looking for a suitable scene to paint, Brown wrote,

> What wonderful effects I have seen
> this eveng in the hay fields, the
> warmth of the uncut grass, the
> greeny greyness of the unmade hay
> in furrows or tufts, with lovely violet
> shadows & long shades of the trees
> thrown athwart all & melting away
> one tint into another imperceptibly, &
> one moment more & cloud passes &
> all the magic is gone.

On 27 July Brown found exactly the place he wanted 'with the full moon behind it just risen' and the next day, in the late afternoon, began to paint it on the spot. He continued this once or twice a week until 24 October, often walking 14 miles (23 kms) a day to do so. In December he worked on the foreground in his studio in Kentish Town, adding the haycart from a study of

floating forms. Whistler's most celebrated works are his *Nocturnes*, twilight views of the Thames which turn it from a dirty trade route, lined with factories, cranes and wharves, into a breathtaking dream world. Whistler's own description, in his *10 O'clock Lecture* of 1885, is the best evocation of his lyrical landscape,

> And when the evening mist clothes
> the riverside with poetry, as with a
> veil, and the poor buildings lose
> themselves in the dim sky, and the
> tall chimneys become campanili, and
> the warehouses are palaces in the
> night, and the whole city hangs in
> the heavens, and fairy-land is before
> us – then the wayfarer hastens home;
> the working man, the cultured one,
> the wise man and the one of
> pleasure, cease to understand, as
> they have ceased to see, and Nature,
> who, for once, has sung in tune,
> sings her exquisite song to the artist
> alone....

The musical analogy in Whistler's titles is very significant. It suggests a function for painting other than as a description of the visible world or as a narrative. Like many other late nineteenth-century artists, Whistler believed that painting could aspire, as the writer Walter Pater said, to 'the condition of music' – that is, it could affect the emotions through form and colour alone. Such thinking, part of the Symbolist reaction against prosaic realism during this period, bears within it the seeds of the abstract art which has flourished this century.

WALTER GREAVES

One of Whistler's most devoted followers was Walter Greaves, the son of a Chelsea boat-builder and waterman. Walter was trained as a shipwright and often painted heraldic devices on the barges belonging to the Lord Mayor and the City of London. With his brother Henry he also painted Chelsea village and the river. Much of his work was influenced by Whistler's *Nocturnes*, although it was usually more prosaic and concerned with the specific details of the Thames; Greaves knew the river as well as Constable knew the Stour.

Greaves's relationship with Whistler is often seen as a tragically dependent one and for many people he is simply the adoring follower who mixed paints and prepared canvases and rowed the great American artist up and down Chelsea Reach in order that he might make sketches.

Whatever the truth of this judgment, there is little doubt that Greaves's masterpiece owes nothing to Whistler. *Hammersmith Bridge on Boat-Race Day* is one of the greatest 'naïve' or 'primitive' paintings to be seen anywhere and was, so the artist claimed, painted when he was 16. It uses bright poster colours which make its Victorian origins almost a mystery. A great crowd of people, many of them precariously perched on sweeping steel cables, watch a racing pair row under the old suspension bridge in west London. There are negro minstrels, clowns, soldiers, sailors and people of all classes, many shown as charming 'wooden-tops'. In their midst are two omnibuses, painted with great concern for their colourful detail: advertisements for Cremorne pleasure gardens and the Oxford Music Hall, and large ornate numbers announcing the fares. Sadly, Greaves was rejected by Whistler in the early 1880s after the latter's bankruptcy following his court case against Ruskin where he won a farthing's damages. Although artists such as Walter Sickert sought

WALTER GREAVES
Hammersmith Bridge on Boat-Race Day
c. 1862 Oil on canvas
91.4 × 139.7 cm
36 × 55 in

to establish Greaves's reputation in later years, he died penniless in 1930.

THE POOL OF LONDON

One of the most dramatic – for some hostile critics, melodramatic – images of the Thames is George Vicat Cole's enormous 10-foot (3-metre) canvas, *The Pool of London,* exhibited in 1888 after ten years of thought and work. It forms part of a series of Thames views which Cole painted in the 1880s for the dealer William Agnew, and shows the area below London Bridge, where Tower Bridge now stands, as the heart of England's maritime and commercial power. Barges and ocean-going steamers on the right and coal barges on the left give the scene an air of activity and, with the choppy water and dark clouds, make the painting a masterpiece of the 'industrial sublime'. The painting was an enormous success and the Prime Minister of the day, W. E. Gladstone, saw in it a rare and remarkable hymn to Britain's industrialized might. He wrote, in 1894, that Cole's picture represented,

> *a scene of commercial activity so as to impress upon it, as I thought, the idea and character of* grandeur. *The picture seemed to speak and to say 'You see here the summit of the commerce of all the world.'*

In contrast to the widespread worship of nature and a rejection of modernity typical of

GEORGE VICAT COLE
The Pool of London
Exhibited 1888
Oil on canvas
189.2 × 304.8 cm
74½ × 120 in

nineteenth-century British art, here is a full-blooded celebration of trade and mechanization on an epic scale. Ironically the vast majority of Cole's paintings were as lyrical and escapist as any of those of his contemporaries. The evasion of such evidently powerful subject matter might serve as the basis of a lengthy discussion of British attitudes to modern society, but it cannot be embarked upon here.

The French painter André Derain painted his version of *The Pool of London* in 1906 during his second visit to London. Many of the Impressionists, such as Claude Monet and Camille Pissarro, had painted in London and were excited by the energy of the river and the grandeur of the surrounding buildings. There was a large market for London scenes in Paris and Derain's picture is one of a series he painted for the dealer Ambrose Vollard, who hoped to cash in on the recent success of Monet's Thames paintings. While Derain shared Cole's excitement at the hustle and bustle of the Pool of London, his approach to the subject and his technique are different. Indeed, a comparison of the paintings allows us to see the shift from traditional to modern art which took place in the late nine-

teenth and early twentieth centuries.

Derain apparently painted his scene from London Bridge, enabling him to take an elevated viewpoint; Cole had painted from water level. Derain's position helps to increase the flattening of the forms and space, particularly in the foreground. Cole's painting uses the full range of traditional techniques of modelling and light effects, whereas Derain's colours are applied in simple planes and create strong contrasts typical, perhaps, of poster designs. These exaggerated colours, derived from an interest in the work of Paul Gauguin, Vincent van Gogh, Paul Cézanne and Georges Seurat, led French critics to call Derain and his colleagues such as Henri Matisse and Maurice Vlaminck *'les fauves'* or 'wild beasts'. This led to a movement called 'Fauvism' in French painting between 1905 and 1907 which, despite its short life, nevertheless exerted an enormous influence on the future development of modern art.

Derain wrote in July 1905 of his 'new conception of light consisting of this: the negation of shadows', a complete contradiction of Cole's method. He also expressed a need to paint 'deliberate disharmonies' as if he were trying to

ANDRÉ DERAIN
The Pool of London
1906 Oil on canvas
65.7 × 99.1 cm
25⅞ × 39 in

THE POST-IMPRESSIONISTS AND THE CAMDEN TOWN GROUP

The term 'post-impressionism', which is used very loosely, was coined by the British critic and painter Roger Fry to describe the work of the French painters he exhibited in two important exhibitions in London in 1910 and 1912. He meant by the term the developments in avant-garde art after the impressionism of Monet, Renoir and others that is to be found in the work of Cézanne, Gauguin and van Gogh. Their work, as well as that of a number of other artists, represented a reaction against the spontaneous 'looseness' of impressionism in favour of a more formalised style. Typically there is an emphasis on geometrical

Walter Sickert 1860-1942

structure and flat often non-naturalistic areas of colour.

The works of those painters who loosely can be termed 'post-Impressionist' were a great inspiration for a group of young British

artists around 1910. An earlier generation, including Philip Wilson Steer and Walter Sickert, had brought to Britain many of the ideas of Impressionist art but balked at the more extreme experiments of Derain, Matisse and their associates in Paris. Spencer Gore, Harold Gilman, Charles Ginner and others founded the Camden Town Group in 1911, with Sickert, who had lived in the area for a number of years, as their mentor. At first the work of the Camden Group showed much in common with the older artist's tonal methods but by 1912 a much more radical and evidently 'modern' approach separates their work from his.

deliver art from worn-out harmonies and emotional dishonesties. The fresh, almost brash areas of red and blue set off against the paler murky greens of the foggy distance reveal a desire to assert the importance of the actual work itself rather than to provide an absolutely accurate representation of the particular place the artist was painting.

THE CAMDEN TOWN GROUP

The Camden Town Group, as the name suggests, was centred on the area north of Euston and south of Chalk Farm which, in the early years of this century, was a poor and distinctly unglamorous district. It was dominated by the great railway cuttings whose construction was so brilliantly described by Charles Dickens, a native of the area, in *Dombey and Son*. As a result of the coming of the railways in the 1850s, formerly respectable terraces were now run-down boarding houses inhabited by the poor, criminals, and, increasingly, young artists. The latter saw in Camden Town a kind of urban version of an artists' colony such as Newlyn in Cornwall (see pages 15–18). They

SPENCER GORE
Houghton Place
1912 Oil on canvas
50.8 × 61 cm
20 × 24 in

wanted to capture the peculiar blend of colour and drabness, destitution and beauty typical of such districts in a style appropriate to this bleak yet seductive new world. Camden Town was also famous for music halls such as the Old Bedford, which at night gave it a lively, bawdy atmosphere in which desperate people found a few hours of explosive and hilarious relief.

Spencer Gore, who had first met Sickert in Dieppe in 1904, was probably the greatest, and certainly the most formally adventurous, of the Camden Town painters; he died young, in March 1914, of pleurisy and pneumonia. He spent a lot of time walking about London and came to love its least fashionable areas, including Camden Town, where he lived at a number of addresses including 2 Houghton Place, Harrington Square. Up to a point he followed Whistler in lending the bare actuality of his chosen scenes a lyrical atmosphere and, as his friend the travelling journalist Ashley Gibson said, 'his artist's eyes saw a violet veil drawn of mornings over the chimney-pots, Victorian facades, and grimy plane trees of Camden Town, and thus he painted them.' Yet Gore's romanticism is by comparison with Whistler's a faint, residual one and his modernist concern with strong formal design and his often dry, scratchy paint surface give his London scenes a raw, matter-of-fact quality.

Gore's Camden Town colleague Charles Ginner used bright, near-Fauvist colours which he applied thickly, creating a patterned, textured surface. His *Piccadilly Circus* (1912) shows one of London's famous landmarks. The view is of part of the surroundings of the statue of Eros, the steps of which are visible on the right. Ginner depicts a few human figures trapped, as it

sense of modernity. The year he painted this work the Italian Futurists held their first exhibition in London; it included multi-coloured images of trains, trams, cars and violent demonstrations. Ginner's picture was probably painted in late 1912 and may have been influenced by the Futurists' dramatic and scandalous work.

ALGERNON NEWTON

There is little feeling of a breathless and motor-dominated metropolis in Algernon Newton's south London scene, *The Surrey Canal, Camberwell* (1935). Newton painted many canal scenes during his career and developed an

ALGERNON NEWTON
The Surrey Canal, Camberwell
1935 Oil on canvas
71.8 × 91.4 cm
28¼ × 36 in

were, between the passing vehicles. Particularly poignant, though this is hardly a sentimental picture, is the figure of the seated flower seller, a familiar character on the London streets. She seems to represent a Victorian past, even, perhaps, a rural world which was fast disappearing in the vortex of modern times.

Ginner uses a snapshot-like composition which accentuates the fleeting and contemporary nature of the scene and paints it in bright, even vulgar, colours which further convey a

eerie classicism of still water, quiet terraces, chimney stacks and calm skies. Newton has been dubbed a modern Canaletto, an artist whose influence he acknowledged. Like Whistler, though in a different, more precise, vein, he found a poetry in his deserted industrial landscapes and frequently invented his views from memory and drawings made in a sketchbook while walking around London. He wrote,

As I walked about London, I saw so much that was worth painting and

GRAHAM SUTHERLAND
*Devastation, 1941: An
East End Street*
1941 Watercolour and
Gouache
64.8 × 113.7 cm
25½ × 44¾ in

*could not be done in any other way,
gleams of sunlight lighting up on
buildings for a few fleeting moments
against a background of pale
clouds. . . . There is beauty to be
found in everything, you only have to
search for it: a gasometer can make
as beautiful a picture as a palace on
the Grand Canal, Venice, it simply
depends on the artist's vision.*

The empty towpath in Camberwell and the
street lamp lighting the dusk scene around it
have a dream-like atmosphere which gives the
painting a surrealist quality. Until quite recently, Newton's work suffered from general
critical neglect on account of its unpretentious
traditionalism of means and stylistic consistency over a long period. Now that technical in-
novation is less highly regarded than it once
was, Newton's art is being reassessed for the
subtle qualities that it undoubtedly possesses.

GRAHAM SUTHERLAND

Graham Sutherland, whose landscapes are
some of the greatest modern images of Wales
(see pages 158–159), was employed as an official
war artist from 1940 to 1945. He painted a
wide range of subjects in different areas, including a series in the East End of London. He

was greatly disturbed by the destruction he saw during the Blitz, yet created from it scenes reminiscent of stage-sets, in which the strange shapes of devastated buildings and twisted metal girders under heavy black skies have a disquieting beauty. It was as if the forces he had discovered in the remote Welsh hillsides were also present in the destructive potential of the German bombs. This is, perhaps, the romance of high explosive.

In May 1941 Sutherland wrote to the Secretary of the War Artists' Advisory Committee that he was immersing himself in the East End and found it 'profoundly interesting and moving'. He later recalled that he became 'tremendously interested in parts of the East End where long rows of terraced houses remained: they were great – surprisingly wide – perspectives of destruction seeming to recede into infinity and the windowless blocks were like sightless eyes.' A huge and seemingly inexplicable worm shape in the distance gives his *Devastation, 1941: An East End Street* a mythological aspect reminiscent of some of Turner's fantastical paintings of legendary beasts.

CAREL WEIGHT

In the 1950s, Carel Weight discovered a very different kind of poetry in the forgotten suburbs of south-west London. *The Dogs* (1955-6) was painted in oil on hardboard from paintings and drawings made outside the old greyhound racing stadium at Wandsworth. Weight wrote of the influence that William Frith's *Derby Day* had on his work that,

> *the actual conception of the people coming out of the Stadium is entirely imaginative as I have never witnessed the scene nor in fact have I ever been there at that time of day. I thought of my picture as a modern counterpoint of Frith's* Derby Day, *a work for which I have the greatest admiration.*

Frith's *Derby Day* is shown on Page 45. Weight's crowd pull away on bicycles and motorbikes and in cars and taxis, or walk home after the evening's entertainment through the dusky streets.

In the sky, near two factory chimneys, a huge orange sun casts an infernal light over the

CAREL WEIGHT
The Dogs
1955-6 Oil on hardboard
122.6 × 243.8 cm
48¼ × 96 in

LEFT: Primrose Hill, from the entrance to London Zoo. It is from approximately this spot that Frank Auerbach painted his view of the hill

shabby scene, almost as if to suggest some kind of imminent or recent tragic event. Weight's later works, still set in London streets, often evoke more explicit dramas with ghostly figures and suggestions of violence or crime. As he has said; 'I like to weave fantasy into mundane things.' In this painting he captures the strange lyricism of anticlimax.

FRANK AUERBACH

Frank Auerbach, who was born in Berlin in 1931, came to England just before the Second World War. He trained under the artist David Bomberg in the 1950s and became his greatest pupil. His work is characterized by thick paint which forms a frequently geometrical framework of brush strokes in and through which images of the real world can be discerned. As in the case of his painting of *Primrose Hill,* Auerbach often rests the picture on each of its edges, painting it from all four sides to ensure a correct distribution of lines and forms. This highly constructive approach is typical of the way in which modern painters conceive of their works as objects with their own life and meaning independent of the subject.

In the late 1960s Auerbach painted three pictures of Primrose Hill, which lies on the north-east side of Regent's Park, near London Zoo. He worked daily on the Tate's painting for over a year, using working drawings made in all seasons and at all times of day from a spot near the zoo entrance, looking up at the hill. The painting in a sense is a record of many different experiences of the same view and the artist explained how it was 'the result of a multiplicity of transmutations partly as the result of external information, alluded to in the drawings, partly as the result of internal intelligences'. Auerbach is able to explain most of the marks on the canvas but not all. Thus he has identified a branch, a path, a lamp-post and a puddle, but is not sure what the orange marks next to the long zigzag of the branch are.

Auerbach has given an intriguing account of the painting's completion,

> *I thought often that I had finished it only to become dissatisfied, and remember as a vivid event the afternoon on which I finally and definitely completed it . . . I thought I had finished it on the day prior to that afternoon. The painting was then almost black. I suddenly realised that I could work on it further. I turned it upside down and finished it the next day.*

FRANK AUERBACH
Primrose Hill
1967-68 Oil on board
121.9 × 146.7 cm
48 × 57¾ in

EAST ANGLIA

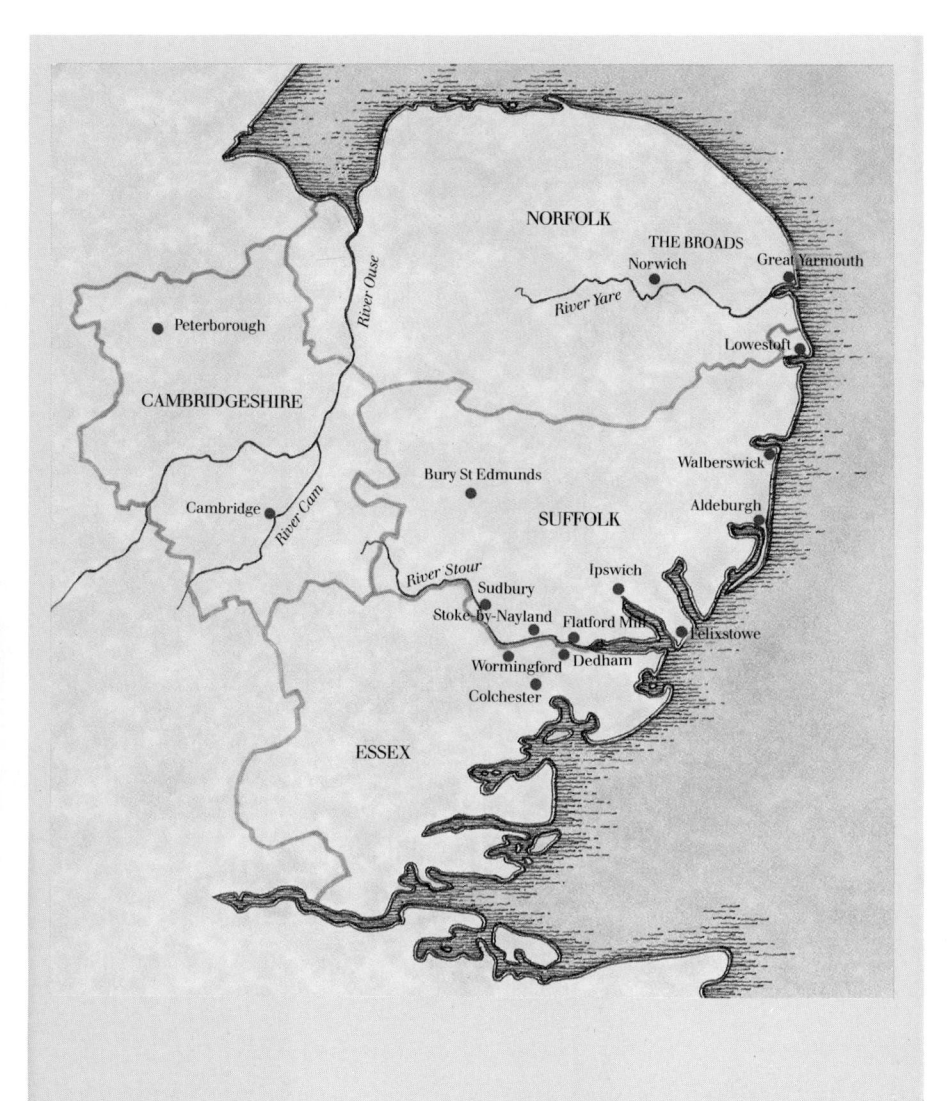

LEFT: Mousehold Heath, once typical of the wide open spaces of the Norfolk countryside (page 86) is now hemmed in on all sides by the urban sprawl of Norwich

East Anglia as a geological region comprises Norfolk, Suffolk and the northern part of Essex. It has traditionally been an isolated area, cut off in medieval times by the undrained fens in the west, the dense oak forests of Essex in the south, and the sea in the north and east.

Even in the eighteenth and nineteenth centuries East Anglia was relatively unindustrialized and, for such a large geographical area, was sparsely populated. East Anglia is mostly lowland, rarely higher than 300 or 400 feet (90-120 metres) above sea level, although it is certainly not uniformly flat as so many people imagine. There is a great variety in the landscape, with rolling fields, and chalk ridges whose loamy soil is especially fertile, making this first-rate country for farming. The Fens, Broads and Breckland are unique areas full of fascinating and varied wildlife, while the coastline with its 'bars', 'nesses' and 'spits' has an unmatched splendour in its constant war with the North Sea.

The two areas chiefly associated with landscape art in East Anglia are the Stour Valley and Norwich. 'Constable Country' lies on the borders of Suffolk and Essex and is one of the most picturesque areas in Britain. It was in fact the home of both Thomas Gainsborough and John Constable and is visited by huge numbers of tourists each year, inspired mostly by Constable's paintings. Further north in Norfolk lies the city of Norwich. In the early nineteenth century Norwich produced a number of fine artists who became known collectively as the Norwich School.

THOMAS GAINSBOROUGH

Thomas Gainsborough was born in the market-town of Sudbury in Suffolk in 1727. His father was a wool weaver, who rebuilt the house which is now open to the public as a museum dedicated to the artist's career. The greater and most successful part of Gainsborough's career was spent in London and Bath as a fashionable portrait painter (see page 11). He was also an enthusiastic amateur musician, with a wide range of friends to whom he wrote letters in an eccentrically brilliant prose, and was regarded by these intimates as a great genius. The actor David Garrick is said to have described him as having a 'cranium so crammed with genius of every kind that it is in danger of bursting upon you, like a steam engine overcharged'.

At the beginning of his career, however, after a period in London in which he was a pupil of

WILLIAM COLLINS
Cromer Sands
1846 Oil on canvas
97.8 × 127 cm
38½ × 50 in
Collins was one of the most popular landscape painters of his time. His often sentimental images of children and dogs painted in a loose, melting style were exactly the kind of paintings Constable opposed his own 'tougher' art to. Actually based on an earlier sketch made at Hastings, this work was painted for the steel pen maker Joseph Gillott and praised by the young Ruskin for its 'truth and solemn feeling'.

THOMAS GAINSBOROUGH
*Landscape with Peasant
on a Path*
1746-7 Oil on canvas
22.2 × 17.1 cm
8¾ × 6¾ in

Much of Gainsborough's creative energy was put into drawing and painting landscapes. This love of the countryside began early in his life and Gainsborough's friend Philip Thicknesse records that,

> during his Boy-hood, though he had
> no idea of becoming a painter then,
> yet there was not a picturesque
> clump of Trees, nor even a single
> Tree of beauty, no, nor hedge row,
> stone or post, at the corner of the
> Lanes, for some miles around about
> the place of his nativity, that he has
> not . . . perfectly in his mind's eye.

These sentiments, which express such a close identification with an area, are very close to those of Constable, who was born in the same region and whose admiration for Gainsborough was so great that he claimed that he saw the master's touch in 'every hedge and hollow tree'.

Some of Gainsborough's first dated works are landscapes, which show his great debt to the seventeenth-century Dutch painters Jacob van Ruysdael, Jan Wijnants and others, whose works he studied in the London salerooms. He also seems to have added figures to some of these old master works for clients who wished to have human interest in their pictures.

Many of Gainsborough's early landscapes are evidently of Suffolk, which he visited from London in the summer months in the 1740s in order to make landscape drawings. It was said that 'Nature was his teacher and the woods of Suffolk his academy' and though this is true in certain respects, his immersion in the old masters also had a profound impact on his landscape vision. It was from them that he learnt the art of harmonious composition, light and shade effects and the means of depicting atmosphere through sky and clouds. His landscapes are extremely artful and although we recognize the essential characteristics of Suffolk in them, yet they have an air about them of being without precise time and place. It is never really possible to locate the views, as is the case with, say, Constable or John Crome. The comparison is apt with Constable, who said that 'with particulars' Gainsborough 'has nothing to do; his object was to deliver a fine sentiment and he has fully accomplished it'.

the Frenchman Hubert Gravelot, Gainsborough spent just over ten years working in Suffolk. Between 1748 and 1752 he worked as a portrait painter in his native Sudbury before moving to Ipswich, where there were many more commissions and where he remained until 1759. Like most painters during this period Gainsborough found that wherever he went the greatest demand was for portraiture. Landscape was in far less demand and it was impossible to make a living out of it. Gainsborough, in spite of his achievements as a portraitist, was inclined to tire of his endless sitters, who paid to be flattered and to have their social status enhanced. The portraitist Sir William Beechey recalled that,

> Gainsborough's landscapes stood
> ranged in long lines from his hall to
> his painting room, and they who
> came to sit for him for their portraits,
> for which he was chiefly employed,
> rarely deigned to honour them with
> a look as they passed them.

NORWICH SCHOOL

Norwich at the turn of the nineteenth century, although to decline in importance, was still a thriving city with a tradition of artistic and intellectual activity. Various societies dedicated to scientific and philosophical study were linked with radical political ideas and gave Norwich the reputation of being anti-establishment.

The city also had an important grouping of amateur and professional painters founded in 1803 called the Norwich Society of Artists. The emphasis in the Society was on sketching from local scenery and on discussion and display of the resulting finished work. Records suggest that the Society was dominated by the drawing masters rather than local dilettanti as was usually the case in most other provincial art

THOMAS GAINSBOROUGH
*Wooded Landscape with
Peasant Resting*
c. 1747 Oil on canvas
62.5 × 78.1 cm
24⅝ × 30¾ in

THE INFLUENCE OF THE DUTCH LANDSCAPISTS

Most of the artists who have worked in East Anglia show an affinity in their work with the Dutch naturalistic landscapists of the seventeenth century. The reasons for this are twofold: first, trade links with the Low Countries were very strong, and the cultural ties between the two areas were correspondingly close; second, the similarities between the landscapes of eastern England and Holland were far greater than with the Mediterranean, which was conventionally the preferred model for British landscape artists.

Jan Wijnants *A Landscape with a Dead Tree and a Peasant Driving Oxen and Sheep Along a Road* 1659 Oil on canvas 80 × 99.4 cm/31½ × 39½ in

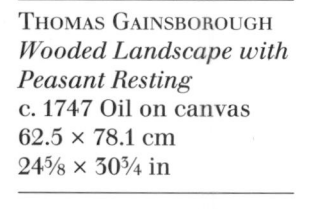

centres. The exhibitions began in 1805 and came to an end in 1833, and were intended to give 'the spur to emulation'. They seem not to have been held with a view to sales, in marked contrast again to the intentions of most other provincial artistic societies. In order to ensure large attendances they were always held in Assize week and the week or two following, and over half the exhibits were usually landscape or other topographical subjects. The self-conscious insularity of the Society may well have helped to give the Norwich School its strong provincial style, evident even in the widely differing outputs of individuals such as John Crome and John Sell Cotman. The Society also developed informal but influential teaching methods and it was this, along with a powerful sense of local identity, which gave the Norwich School an effective life of over thirty years.

Most of the major artists of the school were also closely involved with the city's busy cultural life. However, in spite of this lively milieu, the Norwich School never attracted the kind of local patronage it required and deserved – a fact which exasperated the ambitious and touchy Cotman in particular.

JOHN CROME

The dominant artistic personality of the Norwich School was John Crome, who was born into humble circumstances in 1768, the son of a journeyman weaver and alehouse keeper. After a spell as an apprentice to a sign painter, Crome found a mentor in the person of Thomas Harvey of Catton, a wealthy local weaver who was an amateur artist and collector. Crome was given access to Harvey's collection of old master and contemporary paintings and this allowed him an informal art education as well as a good chance to copy.

Some time in the early 1790s Crome began to sketch local scenery in the company of Robert Ladbrooke, who was also to become a prominent member of the Norwich School. Crome's earliest surviving work dates from 1805, which means that we have no examples from the first fifteen years of his career. Crome apparently first painted after the manner of the great classical landscape painter Richard Wilson (see pages 142–145), whose works, like those of the Dutch masters, he probably first saw in Thomas Harvey's collection. Crome admired Wilson's 'generalizing tendency' (his emphasis, that is, on overall effects of light and shade and unified composition at the expense of precise detail and

local effects). This notion was often justified on the grounds that it made a more immediate by pleasing impression and Crome himself insisted that 'trifles in nature must be overlooked that we may have our feelings raised by seeing the whole picture at a glance, not knowing how or why we are charmed.'

It is worth recalling here that academic theory at this time had made a hierarchy of subject matter: grand historical imagery stood at the top and landscape, along with other popular genres such as still-life and animal painting,

near the bottom. Art's claim to high intellectual status, it was felt, rested on its affinities with great philosophy and literature, and images of fields and rustics were not considered to offer very much scope for the development of such themes.

Landscape painters thus occupied an interesting position in the late eighteenth and early nineteenth centuries. The product they had to offer, in spite of Gainsborough's experience, was increasingly in demand by a large middle-class audience, who often found

the kind of history painting recommended by academic giants such as Sir Joshua Reynolds fairly hard going. Landscape painters therefore sought to satisfy the middle class appetite, while at the same time dignifying their subject matter by introducing literary allusions and giving their compositions the general look and feel of old masters.

In the case of artists such as Crome and other members of the Norwich School, whose images were largely taken from contemporary local sights, the emphasis lay on giving their work the

JOHN CROME
Moonrise on the Yare
c. 1811-16 Oil on canvas
71.1 × 111.1 cm
28 × 43¾ in
Crome's work creates an almost abstract effect of dark silhouettes against the glow of cloudy moonlit sky. Moonlit scenes were popularized in the eighteenth century by the French painter Vernet.

JOHN CROME
*Mousehold Heath,
Norwich*
c. 1818-20 Oil on canvas
109.9 × 181 cm
43¼ × 71¼ in

right 'look'. Crome's collection of old master paintings allowed him constant contact with the appropriate models, the standard by which he would be judged by discerning critics and connoisseurs.

In spite of this classicizing tendency, however, Crome was a painter of a landscape he knew intimately and was always determined to render it in all its specific variety and complexity. Of all the Norwich School artists, he seems to have been most wedded to his environment. One of Crome's most famous and certainly evocative paintings is *Mousehold Heath, Norwich* (1818-20). It shows perfectly what Crome referred to in one of his rare letters as 'one grand plan of light and shade'. Mousehold Heath once extended 8 miles (13 kms) from the old city boundary of Norwich to the Broads by Salhouse, and from the Yare Valley in the south to Rackheath in the north. The Heath still exists as a

public park today, although it is far smaller in its expanse.

Crome's view shows a gently rolling stretch of open heath from between two mounds, with two tracks leading to the horizon which roughly divides the canvas into two halves. On the right-hand mound are two rustic figures, one of whom stands and points towards the distance. This leads our eye across the heath, by way of the tracks, to the high East Anglian sky. Apart from the figures, some cattle in the distance and rather conventional thistle, foxglove and burdock plants in the left foreground, there is little distracting detail in a work which Crome said he had painted chiefly for 'air and space' and for his own pleasure. The breadth and symmetry of the painting certainly create a strong impression of space and freedom and it does seem to have a very private atmosphere about it, as if Crome were making an ideal landscape for his

THE TECHNIQUE OF JOHN CROME

John Crome's complete mastery of aerial perspective (that is, the suggestion of space and depth by means of light and colour) came from his study of certain artists and his own acute observation of real effects occuring in nature. Indeed, his *plein-air* (open-air) effects have often led commentators to view John Crome as an important precursor of the great French Impressionist painters of the second half of the nineteenth century.

Certainly Crome sketched in oil outdoors by 1805, thus anticipating Impressionist

John Crome 1768-1821

method, but like most of his contemporaries Crome most definitely drew a

distinction between a sketch made in front of the subject and the finished work produced in the studio.

The case for John Crome's innovativeness and importance may have been overstated over the years but many of his contemporaries ranked him alongside greats like J. M. W. Turner and John Constable and saw in his particular type of art an extremely remarkable combination of traditional values combined with a thoroughly modern vision and technique.

JOHN SELL COTMAN
The Drop Gate
c. 1826 Oil on canvas
34.9 × 26 cm
13¾ × 10¼ in
Cotman is best-known as a watercolourist yet this superb oil painting shows his enormous talent using a very different technique. The trees are broadly painted which give an extraordinary sense of real space and tangible form. It has been suggested, that the work may have been painted to prove Cotman's critics wrong that he couldn't paint trees.

personal enjoyment only. The depth of the space is typical of Crome's mature work, as are the soft and subtle light values which suffuse every part and help to distance the cloud mass.

As well as being regarded as a great artist John Crome was also held in high esteem as a teacher. It was due directly to his influence that a number of important local painters became known beyond the confines of Norwich. These included James Stark, George Vincent and, perhaps most important of all, Crome's son, John Berney Crome, who also became a teacher and whose energy helped to keep the Norwich Society going during difficult times. Crome's reputation was so high that he suffered many copyists and plagiarists, whose efforts have made a subsequent study of what is in fact a small body of work very difficult.

JOHN SELL COTMAN

The other leading figure of the Norwich School was the watercolour painter John Sell Cotman, who was born in Norwich in 1782, the son of a tradesman. Cotman moved to London in 1798 where he was apparently taken up by the physician Dr Monro, whose patronage had been so beneficial to Turner and Thomas Girtin earlier in the decade. Cotman was very successful in London during these early years, winning a number of awards, exhibiting at the Royal Academy, and making tours of Wales in 1800 and of Yorkshire in 1803. As a prominent member of the Sketching Club he was ranked alongside Turner and Girtin.

Although Cotman was extremely successful and flying high at this stage in his career he made the perhaps odd decision to leave London in 1806 and returned to his native Norwich. Perhaps he was prompted by disappointment at his not being elected to the Society of Painters in Water-Colours that year; it is nevertheless not clear what the reason was for this move but it is one of a number of seemingly strange decisions and events which were to cloud Cotman's life and which have allowed a very real aura of tragedy to surround this, mostly frustrated and embittered artist.

Having been the peer of leading lights in the London art world, Cotman became dominated by a well-meaning but misguided patron, Dawson Turner of Yarmouth, and wasted much of his time and talent on antiquarian etching and on practising as a drawing master to young ladies from well-to-do homes. His last years were spent in London as the head of a family firm which produced drawings for art students to copy. Most sadly of all, perhaps, Cotman, who suffered bouts of severe depression, was unrecognized for most of his life and there is virtually no reference to him in the major art historical sources of the time. This represents a remarkable decline for an artist who has been hailed by some as one of the greatest watercolourists of all time.

A very fine example of Cotman's art from the period soon after he returned to Norwich is the view of a bustling *Norwich Market Place,* which was close to his birthplace in the parish of St Mary Coslany. Cotman is best known for his country views, yet here we can see his brilliant talent for organizing complex detail into beautifully clear and differentiated areas of colour. There was also a definite significance in the view for a contemporary audience. Britain's survival of the wars with France was not only seen as a result of her military and naval powers but also her economic strength. The thriving market place, where a number of soldiers can be seen, would have given a reassuring image of a country whose domestic resources were fully capable of sustaining her struggles abroad. Turner's famous painting of Leeds of 1816 (Yale

JOHN SELL COTMAN
Norwich Market Place
c. 1806 Watercolour
40.6 × 64.8 cm
16 × 25½ in

CONSTABLE – A MAN AHEAD OF HIS TIME

Turner, his great rival, was made a Royal Academician by the age of 27. Constable only achieved that status in 1829 when he was 53. While Turner might easily make thousands of pounds a year (he died a millionaire), Constable only ever made a very modest income from sale of his work. The whole problem rested on Constable's attitude to the 'finish' of a picture. In order to achieve the effects for which he is now so admired Constable applied paint in a radically new fashion which just did not suit contemporary taste. A Regency eye demanded smooth, idealized images whether they be of people,

J. M. W. Turner 1775-1851

John Constable 1776-1837

historical scenes or landscapes. Time and again Constable presented works for exhibition that seemed both to the public and to most of his fellow artists rough and unfinished.

Today, however, millions of people know and love works such as *The Haywain* in the National Gallery or the Tate's *Scene on a Navigable River (Flatford Mill).* But when these great

works were exhibited in London they frequently met with what Constable had sadly come to expect – scorn and adverse criticism. In Paris, however, Constable's paintings were greeted with praise and astonishment. Artists of the stature of Eugène Delacroix were thrilled by Constable's revolutionary techniques and stunning colour, and Parisian critics hailed their 'general vivacity and richness'. Once again, the French can be seen responding with quite acute sensitivity to an exciting new art, while the British just stare in disbelief and ridicule.

JOHN CONSTABLE
Stoke-by-Nayland
c. 1810-11 Oil on canvas
18.1 × 26.4 cm
7⅛ × 10⅜ in

Center for British Art, Mellon Collection, United States of America) had a similar message. Some understanding of British artists' patriotic interest in the war and the country's economic health can be gained by reading the diaries of the painter and diarist Joseph Farington.

JOHN CONSTABLE

John Constable was, by his own account, a failure. To a twentieth-century eye this may seem almost incredible. Was it really possible to paint works such as *Scene on a Navigable River (Flatford Mill)* or *The Glebe Farm* and not receive ample reward in terms of money and reputation? The simple fact was that Constable's pictures were not popular due mainly to the particular technique by which Constable applied paint to canvas. Where we may see a

brilliant manipulation of paint to organize fresh and vivid natural scenes, Constable's general audience saw awkwardness, even charlatanism. Turner suffered similar criticism for his later works, but Constable met opposition throughout most of his career. Each major work he produced caused him ever-increasing anxiety as he struggled to stay true to his vision and yet make a painting which would have the grand scope and scale expected at the Academy.

Like Turner, Constable wished to elevate landscape's status within the hierarchy of subject matter; unlike Turner, he never painted historical landscapes. Although he admired Claude Lorraine and Nicolas Poussin as much as any painter, he steadfastly refused to imitate those great masters. Although Constable was by temperament and upbringing extremely conservative in his cultural and political views, he was a radical in art. He wished to paint the Stour Valley he had loved since boyhood in order to give 'a pure and unaffected representation'.

Constable accepted from a very early date that there could be no easy way of achieving his aims. His dogged application to what must often have seemed a terrible chore can be sensed in a letter he wrote to his friend John Dunthorne in 1802. Good painting, he asserted,

can only be obtained by long contemplation and incessant labour in the executive part... The great vice of the present day is bravura, an attempt at something beyond the truth. In endeavouring to do something better than well they do what in reality is good for nothing. Fashion *always has, and will have its day – but* Truth *(in all things) only will last and can have just claims on posterity.*

As an artist, Constable's great strength lay in his single-minded determination to express the truth of what he saw. He never travelled abroad, a rare thing for an artist of his day, and spent much of his career painting the countryside where he had been born in 1776. He was the second son of Golding Constable, who was an extremely wealthy and influential corn and coal merchant of East Bergholt in the Dedham Vale. The mills owned by Constable's father, most famously Flatford Mill, became some of the most important motifs in the artist's work.

Constable at first worked in the family business and painted in his spare time. Eventually,

JOHN CONSTABLE
Dedham Lock and Mill
c. 1819 Oil on canvas
54.6 × 76.5 cm
21½ × 30⅛ in
This shows the Constables' other mill, at Dedham, from the Suffolk bank of the Stour, looking southwards. The painting is unfinished to the right and allows us to see the red-brown ground on which Constable builds up his effects. It is not clear why this work was never finished.

however, and in spite of his father's opposition, Constable entered the Royal Academy in 1799, where he was given great encouragement by the painter and collector Sir George Beaumont. Beaumont, who supported Constable's career throughout his life, had a superb collection of paintings which he allowed the young artist to copy and which helped to form his notion of great art. However, while Constable recognized the importance of learning from the great art of the past, his first model was always, and of necessity, nature. He later wrote,

The world is wide; no two days are alike, nor even two hours; neither were there ever two leaves of a tree alike since the creation of the world; and the genuine productions of art, like those of nature, are all distinct from each other.

found the Lake District oppressive because in his view it lacked human associations, quite unfashionably followed the path taken by provincial painters such as those in Norwich and Bristol. Unlike many of those artists, however, he also constantly brought to the spectator's attention the agricultural and economic reality of a scene.

This vision of the landscape is expressed with great force in *Scene on a Navigable River (Flatford Mill)* painted in 1816 and 1817 and exhibited at the Academy in 1817 where it failed to sell. It is the prototype of the famous series of 6-foot (2-metre) canvases which Constable began to exhibit two years later and in which he invested so much of his time and nervous energy. It is almost certainly the work seen by Farington on 2 January 1817 when the painter and diarist

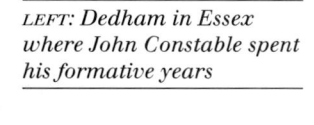

LEFT: Dedham in Essex where John Constable spent his formative years

For the first ten years of his career as a painter Constable divided his time between London and Suffolk. His deep love of the Stour Valley was tied to a profound understanding of it as a working human landscape. Many landscape artists in Constable's lifetime effectively ignored the human presence in the views they painted, preferring to offer images within the conventional categories of 'picturesque', 'beautiful' and 'sublime'. Frequently, moreover, they chose to paint scenery with a romantic or exotic appeal, such as Wales, the Lake District or Continental subjects. Their appeal was to a market increasingly determined by the desire for escape from the cities and tourism. Constable, who actually

wrote that he had called on Constable 'to look at several painted studies from nature made by him last summer & autumn; also a large landscape composed of the Scenery at Dedham in Essex. I exhorted him to compleat them.'

The view taken is from the slightly elevated slope of the southern end of the Flatford footbridge looking up the towpath to Golding Constable's lock and mill. In the foreground a young boy sits astride a towing horse, which is being disconnected from some barges prior to their being poled under the bridge. The horse would then cross the bridge and be reharnessed to the barges in order to continue towing on the other bank. A stream divides the path from the field on the right where a farm worker is shown carrying a large scythe. The time of day, as the shadows reveal, is noon. The paint is applied in a varied texture which has a kind of tangible quality, allowing us to feel the three-dimensional reality of trees and plants, and the plastic quality of sky, clouds and water. The atmosphere is thick with the heat of a summer's midday, the buzzing of insects and flight of clouds of pollen. This was one of Constable's first major efforts at what he called 'natural painture'.

There are various drawings and oil studies going back to 1814 which relate to this painting. It is notoriously hard, however, to disentangle the complexities of Constable's working methods by examining such evidence. He made great numbers of pencil and oil sketches and seems to have used them at will, often many years later, in the process of making a finished canvas. One result of this is that Constable's landscapes became apparently timeless. Actual changes in the scenery are not recorded and one is left with a distinct impression that, for all its freshness and vivacity, Constable's landscape was in many senses a nostalgic one. It is in part an attempt by the artist to recapture the countryside as he knew it in his youth – before his own troublesome maturity and before the social, economic and agricultural changes that were already altering his beloved Stour Valley.

In 1821, in a famous passage, Constable wrote with great feeling to his friend and confidant John Fisher,

But the sound of water escaping from Mill dams, so do willows, Old rotten Banks, slimy posts, & brickwork. I love such things. . . As long as I do paint I shall never cease to paint such places. They

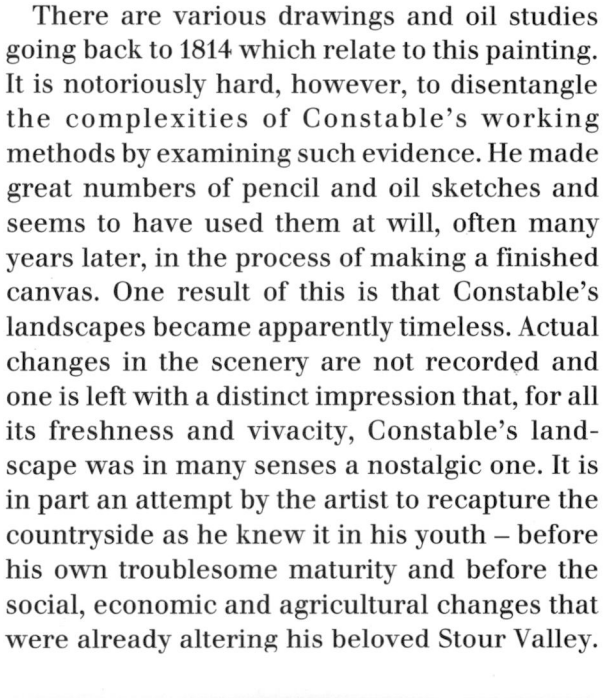

ABOVE: Flatford Mill, Suffolk – a view taken from across the River Stour

have always been my delight. . . But I should paint my own places best – Painting is but another word for feeling. I associate my 'careless boyhood' to all that lies on the banks of the Stour. They made me a painter (and I am gratefull), that is I had often thought of pictures of them before I ever touched a pencil.

Just over ten years after *Scene on a Navigable River (Flatford Mill)* we find Constable in an utterly changed mood. His *Sketch for Hadleigh Castle* shows an empty ruin which commands a view over the Thames Estuary towards the Kent hills and out into the Channel.

Where *Scene on a Navigable River (Flatford Mill)* showed an enclosed working landscape

JOHN CONSTABLE
Scene on a Navigable River (Flatford Mill)
1816-17 Oil on canvas
101.6 × 127 cm
40 × 50 in

on a hot summer's day in rich greens agreeably picked out with warm spots of red, here we are given an early morning view in cold and stormy weather of a desolate and melancholy seascape. The man and dog in the left foreground are dwarved by the castle ruins and even seem lost under a threatening sky in which a few birds hover on the wind. The entire surface of the canvas is covered with rough patches and streaks of impasted white paint (impasted paint is paint which has been applied thickly in order to create a textured surface) which give the painting's surface a life of its own, independent of the image described. Compared with the finished painting exhibited in 1829, the sketch has a dark, brooding presence which seems to suggest some sense of loss or death. This is a wasteland where human effort becomes unreal and meaningless.

The painting almost certainly reflects Constable's devastation and consequent severe depression after the death of his wife Maria in November 1828. Constable's friend John Fisher had suggested to the artist that he overcome his grief by throwing himself into work on a major canvas and assured him that 'some of the finest works of art have been the result of periods of distress.' It seems very likely, therefore, that *Hadleigh Castle* fulfilled this need. This assess-

ment needs qualifying, however, by considering the painting in the context of Constable's work of the late 1820s and early 1830s. His art had become more 'expressionist', to use what is strictly speaking a twentieth-century term, as the 1820s wore on. His handling of paint was looser, he showed greater interest in dramatic weather effects and, as can be seen in his views of Hampstead for instance, he was increasingly concerned with grand and even sublime views. The sky, Constable believed, was the chief 'organ of sentiment' in landscape painting and it virtually becomes the subject matter of many of his pictures. Architecture also seems to have gained in importance for him, although he had always been fascinated by dwellings in the landscape as images of man's life and condition.

Just as Turner had given his classical ruins a symbolic and metaphorical role – alluding to the aspirations of man and the frailty of his achievements – so Constable used buildings for their poetic resonance. Following a familiar device of romantic poetry, *Hadleigh Castle* becomes what the writer T. S. Eliot would later come to call an 'objective correlative' for Constable's feelings: *he* is the castle, empty and ruined on the edge of the civilized world.

Conservative as he was, Constable also sought in his later works to express a sense of

JOHN CONSTABLE
Sketch for Hadleigh Castle
c. 1828-9 Oil on canvas
122.6 × 167.3 cm
48¼ × 65⅞ in

JOHN CONSTABLE
The Valley Farm
1835 Oil on canvas
147.3 × 125.1 cm
58 × 49¼ in

concern about the world around him with its land enclosures and new machinery. The agricultural riots in Suffolk in the early 1820s had shaken his faith in the natural order of society and he felt increasingly threatened by the likelihood of change and chaos.

It is no surprise then to find Constable moving from rather fraught emotions to the withdrawn nostalgia of his frankly picturesque views of the Glebe and Valley farms in the early 1830s. Valley Farm was a favourite subject for Constable and he painted it on many occasions throughout his career. It is the building in *The Haywain* and occurs more often in Constable's works than even Flatford Mill. The surface of the painting seems overworked and it has been suggested by more than one art historian that this shows Constable's almost frantic attempt to make the past real.

There is little doubt that works such as this and *The Glebe Farm*, showing a similar building at Langham, were fantasies of a kind intended to deny present circumstances and to offer escape into a pastoral idyll. In many respects there are affinities to be found here with the visionary landscapes of Shoreham in Kent painted by Samuel Palmer and the 'Ancients' – the nineteenth-century group of artists inspired

J. M. W. TURNER
Aldeburgh
Engraved 1827
Watercolour
27.9 × 40 cm
11 × 15¾ in

BELOW: The fishing village of Walberswick in Suffolk became the centre for an artists' colony in the second half of the nineteenth century

by the works and philosophy of the painter and visionary William Blake.

PHILIP WILSON STEER

The small fishing village of Walberswick in Suffolk became popular with artists in the second half of the nineteenth century. Turner had spotted the picturesque qualities of this stretch of the coast earlier when he painted his watercolour of men salvaging a ship's mast in the harbour at Aldeburgh, a few miles south of Walberswick. The famous illustrator of *Punch*, Charles Keene, made many drawings and etchings of the coast near Walberswick in the 1860s and 1870s. The marine painters Henry Moore and T. Irving Dalgleish also painted there in the 1870s and 1880s. By the 1880s Walberswick had become an artists' colony just as Newlyn and St Ives had in Cornwall.

Philip Wilson Steer, who was born in Birkenhead in 1860, is perhaps the most important painter associated with Walberswick and the surrounding area where he had friends. He had

THE CITY EXODUS

Following the example of French painters who had gone to live and work in small villages in Brittany, many British painters began to look for 'authentic' settings in this country. In many cases their desire was to get away from the city and to discover what they felt must be a more natural, less pretentious way of life in a pre-industrial setting. These, of course, had been the ideals of many artists before, such as Samuel Palmer and the 'Ancients' in

Shoreham, Kent, and they are a key feature of the Romantic tradition in European art.

The artist's life is seen in this view as an ideal one in which imagination, desire and practise come together in a way impossible for most people in their routine work-dominated lives in the city. The artist's colony, itself derived from the monastic tradition and early anarchist groups, was a forerunner of the hippy communes of the 1960s.

trained in Paris in the early 1880s and came under the influence of the French Impressionist painters and, in particular, of the American painter J. A. M. Whistler.

Steer's art was an original, if idiosyncratic, version of the new developments in French art. Traces of the work of Edouard Manet, Claude Monet, Camille Pissarro and Georges Seurat can be found in his views of young girls enjoying the sea and air, painted on his frequent visits to Suffolk in the 1880s. On these visits he stayed first at the inn on the village green and then at Valley Farm on the edge of Walberswick.

The Beach at Walberswick shows three young women standing on the pier looking out to sea across a curving shingle bank. Steer paints (quite thinly) over an ochre ground and adds separate touches of red, yellow and blue in a manner which suggests his knowledge of Seurat's *pointilliste* technique (*pointilliste* is a technique of creating light effects by filling an area

PHILIP WILSON STEER
The Beach at Walberswick
c. 1889 Oil on canvas
60.3 × 76.2 cm
23¾ × 30 in

PHILIP WILSON STEER
Girls Running:
Walberswick Pier
c. 1884-94 Oil on canvas
62.9 × 92.7 cm
24¾ × 36½ in

with tiny dots of various colours). His figures seem to melt into the atmosphere and have an almost naïve reality, in keeping, perhaps, with his view of the subject. Steer's personal variation on Impressionism, his frequently abstract sense of colour and his doll-like figures caused problems for many critics at the time. While they could appreciate the effects of light and atmosphere, the means by which these were achieved seemed to a conventional eye clumsy and even grotesque. The hovering figures and the simple sweeping curve of the beach also show a relationship with French and Belgian symbolist painting of the period.

This is even more evident in Steer's remarkable *Girls Running: Walberswick Pier* (1888-94), which shows signs of considerable reworking in the varied, broken texture. The insubstantial figures casting long shadows as they loom up before us have a positively dream-like quality, almost as if they are spectres. It seems likely in fact that Steer painted this work from memory, for the pier-head is on the opposite side to that shown in *The Beach at Walberswick*, while the shingle bank is the same. Steer made many annotated pencil, watercolour and oil sketches which provided him with material for final works which always have a strong element of reverie about them. Steer's themes are female innocence, freedom and beauty seen in the shimmering light of an unspoilt coastline. It was a vision with a strong appeal to a contemporary audience, even if Steer's methods occasionally raised a few eyebrows.

JOHN NASH

The leading East Anglian landscape painter of the twentieth century has been John Nash, the younger brother of that other great landscape artist Paul Nash. Although born in London, Nash lived in the Stour Valley from 1929 until his death. He had become fond of the east coast in 1912, when he made a walking tour in Norfolk with the artist Claughton Pellew-Harvey, who also gave him some tuition in painting. After living in the Chilterns and at Princes Risborough in the 1920s, Nash and his wife, Christine, moved to Wormingford in Essex in 1929 and finally settled in a simple very attractive cottage

JOHN NASH
Wild Garden, Winter
1959 Watercolour
40.6 × 57.1 cm
16 × 22½ in

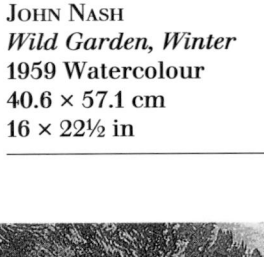

RIGHT: Bottengoms, John Nash's cottage at Wormingford in Essex

called Bottengoms at the end of the Second World War.

Bottengoms, whose name apparently derives from that of a Saxon farmer, is a two-storeyed sixteenth-century building of wood and plaster with just three main rooms with low ceilings; above these rooms are two bedrooms, and an L-shaped studio with a view over the Stour Valley from which Nash painted many of his great landscapes.

Nash lived an extremely simple life for many years, managing without electricity or conventional running water – his water source was a stream which ran along an open culvert in his kitchen. Nash, who was also a superb botanical illustrator, cultivated a remarkable garden at Wormingford which can be seen in many of his

paintings. His art is pre-eminently that of a countryman who understands as well as loves the things he depicts. Although he painted landscapes in all parts of Britain in the course of his life, it was the Stour Valley that captured his imagination the most. He told Sir John Rothenstein, a former Director of the Tate Gallery, that, when compared with western Britain, the East Anglian atmosphere was 'more brilliant ... subtler, less obviously dramatic'.

It is this quiet subtlety that pervades Nash's work. His style hardly changed throughout his career, and his consistent aim was to capture a sense of place in a style notable for its logic and simplicity. This simplicity is not that of a *faux-naif*, pretending to be unsophisticated; rather it is the result of a quiet mastery of both his own

perceptions and his artistic means. Carel Weight, the painter, remembered that Nash 'never worked feverishly, however urgent the need to complete a picture, but in a calm, easy-going way'. Nash evidently aimed at a tranquil sense of order in all his work and he explained to Rothenstein that in looking at a landscape 'its abstract features appeal pretty quickly. Although representational I am primarily interested in the structure underneath, though I hope not obviously.'

Like his predecessors Gainsborough, Constable, Cotman and Crome, Nash found in the East Anglian landscape an understated grandeur which transcended mere physical features and could be arrived at only by a slow meditative approach.

JOHN NASH
Mill Building, Boxted
1962 Oil on canvas
71.1 × 81.3 cm
28 × 32 in
Painted in the late summer and autumn of 1962, the view is of a stretch of the river Stour in Essex with the backs of old mill buildings on the right. The mill has subsequently been demolished.

THE
HEART OF ENGLAND

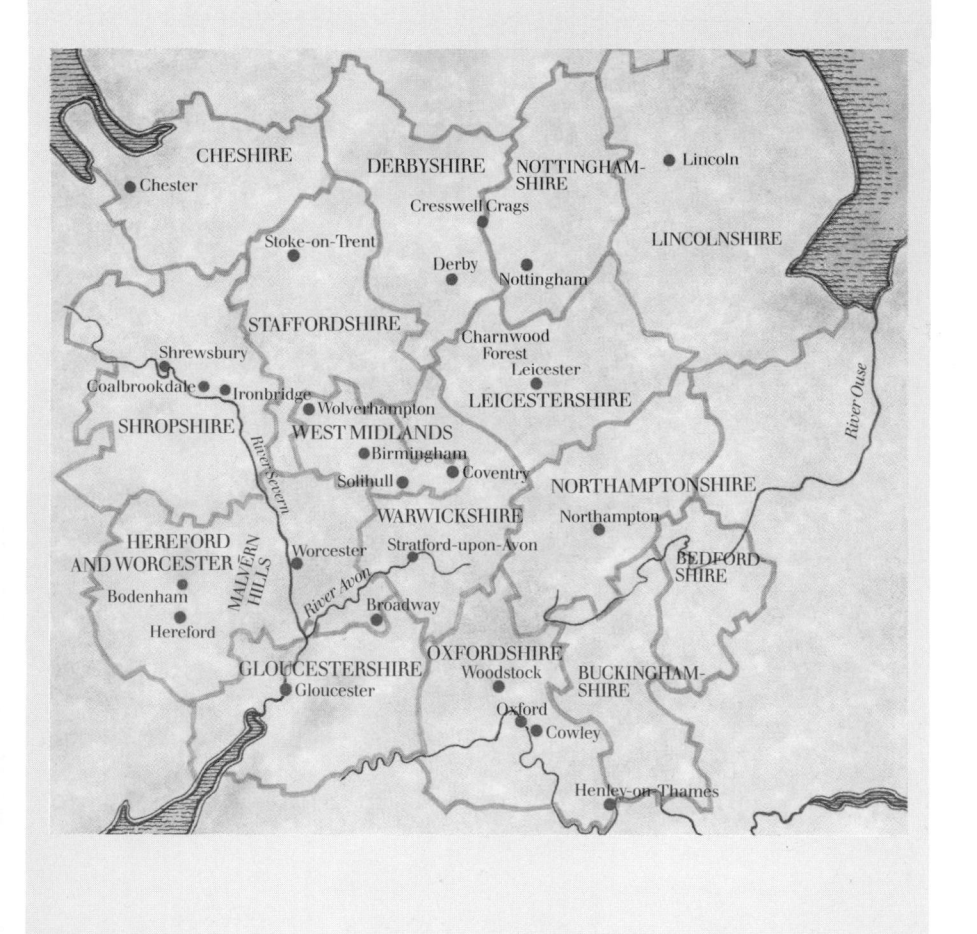

LEFT: The Malvern Hills, Herefordshire, seen in panoramic fashion in John Varley's view of Bodenham and the Malvern Hills, Herefordshire 1801 (page 109)

The phrase 'Heart of England' brings to mind both centrality and core. The Midlands are dominated by the huge industrialized sprawl of Birmingham and the surrounding manufacturing towns which made such an important contribution to Britain's economic supremacy in the nineteenth century. For those connected with the great enterprise of that period, Heart of England was an appropriate label, but of course that is hardly the usual sense in which it is used. For the majority of people it suggests an area somewhere between Oxford and Nottingham, Shrewsbury and Peterborough, which is rich in arable land, meandering valleys and deep forest and woodland.

The Heart of England is for many 'Shakespeare Country', conjuring up an image of half-timbered cottages and haywagons and, by association with the great playwright, a romantic mixture of the events of British history and the dream world of *As You Like It*. This is not to deny that a number of artists have responded to the industrial world of the Midlands. It is largely true, however, that a rather picturesque or romanticized view of this new environment has dominated. The fascination with Ironbridge, for instance, has derived in the main from its superb natural setting and the almost Gothic quality of its buildings, which in any case fell into disuse and decay quite quickly after its heyday as an industrial centre.

JAN SIBERECHTS AND EARLY BRITISH LANDSCAPE

A notable early British landscape is Jan Siberechts' view of Henley-on-Thames, painted about 1690. Siberechts was one of a number of foreign artists who practised landscape painting in Britain in the late seventeenth century.

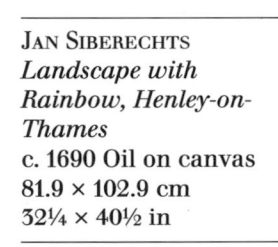

JAN SIBERECHTS
Landscape with Rainbow, Henley-on-Thames
c. 1690 Oil on canvas
81.9 × 102.9 cm
32¼ × 40½ in

JOHN WOOTTON
George Henry Lee, 3rd Earl of Litchfield and his uncle the Hon. Robert Lee, subsequently 4th Earl of Litchfield, shooting in 'True Blue' Frockcoats
1744 Oil on canvas
203.8 × 245.1 cm
80¼ × 96½ in

This was the period when a recognizably modern world of art developed, with dealers, auctioneers and writers on art becoming familiar to a middle- and upper-class audience. Artists began to specialize in their output in order to cater for particular markets such as portraiture, still life, sporting pictures and landscape. Siberechts, who was born in Antwerp, came to England in about 1672 to benefit from the expanding market and painted a number of important country house views, including two of Longleat in Wiltshire in 1675 and 1676. Before his death, however, which occurred some time between 1700 and 1703, Siberechts' work became highly naturalistic and shows an almost scientific concern with the effects of light and atmosphere, as well as an interest in the working aspects of the landscape.

The view of Henley sets the houses and church of the small town under a wooded hill and a dark stormy sky with an eye-catching double rainbow. Boats loaded with cargo can be seen moving up the river or anchored along a towpath. In the foreground horses, sheep and farm labourers dominate the meadow, while on the right a milkmaid sits and milks one of her herd. It is the scenery described by Celia Fiennes, who toured Britain between 1685 and 1705, and who commented rapturously in her journal on the economic growth of Britain into an 'island workshop', where rivers were the arteries of trade and fields the source of new cultivation. Fiennes believed it was important for Britons to appreciate their own country and that a tour 'would form such an idea of England, add much to its Glory and Esteem in our minds and cure the itch of over-valuing foreign parts'. This is one of the first important statements about the attractions of Britain for the tourist. Natural beauty was less a concern at this stage, however, than the pleasure and instruction to be gained from observing a nation 'pushing and improving', as Daniel Defoe put it, going on to assert through the voice of a 'wondrous' foreigner that 'England was not like other's countrys, but it was all a planted garden.'

JOHN WOOTTON

While Siberechts painted a landscape nurtured and maintained by the 'pushing' of the middle classes, others depicted a traditional one of

great estates and aristocratic sport. John Wootton dominated sporting and landscape art in England during the first half of the eighteenth century. His patrons included George II and Frederick, Prince of Wales, as well as many of the great titled landowners of the time, such as the Dukes of Devonshire, Newcastle and Beaufort. Wootton had an instinctive grasp of the interests and passions of his clients and made images of them as the proud and natural rulers of the land. Little is known about Wootton's early life, except that he was born in Warwickshire and studied under the Dutch landscape painter John Wyck before moving to London in about 1700. He was a skilful and versatile

painter who was adept at using a variety of styles to suit his wide-ranging subject matter. He painted battle, hunting and racing scenes, horses, dogs, country houses and both classical and topographical landscapes.

Wootton's large painting of George Henry Lee and his uncle Robert Lee on a shooting trip shows the Arcadian and poetical quality he brought to his hunting landscapes. The two men carry double-barrelled flintlock shotguns and have been out with their three pointers whose collars show they belong to Robert Lee. It is likely that the two leading figures' heads are the work of a professional portrait painter rather than Wootton who frequently collaborated with other artists. On the left a game-keeper stands by a pheasant they have shot and a groom waits on the right. The luxuriant setting is probably in Dichley Park, which was the Lees' seat as Earls of Litchfield, near Woodstock in Oxfordshire.

An interesting point about the Lees' dress is that they are shown wearing the 'True Blue' coats adopted by supporters of Bonnie Prince Charlie, the Young Pretender and leader of the Stuart cause. They were therefore both traitors, in the eyes of the Hanoverians, and would have

elevated to the 'grand style' demanded by contemporary taste. It was this fusion of the high and low which irritated Constable, who said of Wootton that he 'painted country gentlemen in their wigs and jockey caps, and placed them in Italian landscapes resembling Gaspar Poussin, except in truth and force'. This reaction shows very clearly the change in taste that took place between the two artists' lifetimes. During Wootton's career landscape painting was expected to follow social as well as artistic conventions; for Constable and many of his contemporaries,

LEFT: *Cresswell Crags on the Nottinghamshire and Derbyshire border. The Crags provided the dramatic backdrop for* Horse Devoured by a Lion *by George Stubbs 1763*

GEORGE STUBBS
Horse Devoured by a Lion
1763 Oil on canvas
69.2 × 103.5 cm
27¼ × 40¾ in

suffered the disappointment of the failure of the Forty-Five Rebellion, the last Jacobite uprising, which took place the year after the picture was painted. There are evidently political overtones to the work, which shows two men who believe in their God-given right to the land and its bounties. Wootton shows George Henry Lee mounted on his horse and holding his riding whip as if it were a commander's baton. This is a ritualized and proprietorial landscape which exudes an air of belief in the rightness of the social order. This 'rightness' was a theme of the Tory writers who were Wootton's friends and admirers – Alexander Pope, Jonathan Swift and John Gay. Wootton probably advised Pope on the design of his villa and garden at Twickenham and shared with him a profound taste for the classical tradition in the arts. This classicism is evident in the Italianate aspect of the painting of the Lees' shooting trip: the distant landscape is idealized with ruins and a 'Claudian' soft horizon (after the classical style of the seventeenth-century French painter Claude Lorraine). Wootton displays here his sure sense of the way in which a sporting picture can be

such conventions were irrelevant to the artist's true depiction of a natural landscape.

GEORGE STUBBS

George Stubbs, the great animal painter, painted a sequence of works in the 1760s showing a lion attacking a horse. Legend had it that Stubbs witnessed such an event in North Africa while returning from Italy in the early 1750s. There is no real evidence for this anecdote and it is almost certain that Stubbs's inspiration for the theme, of which there are seventeen known paintings, was an antique marble sculpture. Stubbs could have seen this either in the Palazzo dei Conservatori in Rome or, in reproduction, in Britain, possibly at Ince Blundell Hall, the home of one of his patrons. Stubbs divides the whole episode into four parts, showing the horse aware of the lion's presence as it emerges from its cave; the horse frozen with fear; the lion having sprung on the horse's back; and the horse collapsed to the ground under the lion's weight.

Almost without doubt the setting is Cresswell

STUBBS AND THE SUBLIME

George Stubbs was a brilliant draughtsman whose knowledge of the structure of animals was based not only on close external study but also on his anatomical dissections. The first series of paintings dealing with the famous lion and horse theme was exhibited in 1763 and led the writer Horace Walpole to compose a poem based on it which describes the horse's 'apprehension, horror, hatred, fear', with its

George Stubbs 1724-1806

'ears shot forward' and 'stiff, projected mane'. Walpole's language shows that he appreciated the sublime quality of Stubbs's paintings, which are some of the first Romantic images in European art. A contemporary audience, following artistic categories of the day, would have read the lion as a 'sublime' creature on account of its wildness and power and the horse as 'beautiful' in its grace and nobility.

for an increasing amount of visitors.

Stubbs's friend the miniaturist Ozias Humphry recorded that the horse in the paintings was 'painted from one of the King's horses in the Mews wch. Mr. Payne the Architect procur'd for him – The expression of this produced, repeatedly, from time to time by pushing a brush apon the ground towards him'. Humphry also states that the lion in the Stubbs' picture was based on observations of a lion in Lord Shelburnes's menagerie at Hounslow Heath where Stubbs made a great many pencil drawings.

Crags on the Nottinghamshire and Derbyshire borders about 2 miles (3 kms) from Welbeck Abbey. Stubbs may well have visited the Crags first in 1762 while working 20 miles (32 kms) away at Wentworth Woodhouse for the Marquess of Rockingham, for whom he produced a number of important horse paintings. The Crags are two opposing ranges of high limestone cliffs, irregular in shape and overhung with trees, plants and bushes. This impressive gorge has the shallow River Wellow running through it and is distinguished by a notched effect in the magnesium limestone which can be clearly seen in Stubbs's painting of the area. It was not until 1874 that professional archaeologists excavated the Crags and discovered the remains of horses, bison, woolly rhinoceri, hyenas and cave lions, as well as evidence of prehistoric man's inhabitation of the various caves. We cannot be sure, therefore, what Stubbs knew about the Crags, which were a very remote spot in the eighteenth century and on none of the early picturesque itineraries of writers such as William Gilpin. It is quite likely, however, that he could have come across bones and other remains while sketching in the area and that these led him to imagine the lion's attack. James Ward's *Gordale Scar* (see page 133), painted fifty years later, also uses a prehistoric site with wild animals to evoke an awesome, primitive atmosphere. Even in the 1760s Stubbs would not have been alone in being fascinated by the archaeological suggestiveness of the scenery at Creswell Crags and in responding to its 'sublimity'. There was a definite interest during this period not only in remote parts of the British landscape but also in its prehistory, and knowledge of a distant, pre-human past lent these remote areas a mysterious power which added greatly to their attraction

JOHN VARLEY

John Varley, brother of the watercolourist and scientist Cornelius Varley (see pages 149–150), was born in London in 1778 and was at first trained as a portrait painter. By 1796 he was sketching in and around London and in 1798 went on a tour to Peterborough which confirmed him as a landscape artist. At this time Varley came into contact with Dr Monro, the patron of many landscape painters in watercolour, and attended his famous 'evenings' at the Adelphi in London as well as visiting his country house in Fetcham, Surrey.

Between 1798 and 1802 Varley toured Wales and Herefordshire extensively, making drawings out of doors which often used the broad 'panoramic' view found in *View of Bodenham and the Malvern Hills, Herefordshire* of 1801. There is a concern for geographical accuracy in the work which is characteristic of English *plein-air* (open-air) painting of the period, as well as an interest in particular weather conditions and times of the day. This scientific attitude is perhaps ironic for an artist who was totally obsessed with the astrological analysis of human character!

THE INDUSTRIAL LANDSCAPE

In the very first years of the nineteenth century

JOHN VARLEY
View of Bodenham and the Malvern Hills, Herefordshire
1801 Watercolour
31.1 × 52.1 cm
12¼ × 20½ in

John Sell Cotman lived at 107 New Bond Street, the home and business premises of the stationers and print sellers William and James Munn. In the back parlour on the first floor their brother, the watercolourist Paul Sandby Munn, turned out drawings for sale in the shop. Munn's godfather was the great topographical draughtsman Paul Sandby, one of the pioneers of British landscape watercolour painting. Cotman also worked in New Bond Street with Munn, producing drawings for the market among amateurs, mostly ladies, who used them a great deal as drawing-copies.

Munn and Cotman toured North Wales together in the summer of 1802 and before they crossed the border they visited Coalbrookdale, where they both drew the famous iron bridge constructed by Abraham Darby between 1774 and 1781. They were fascinated by the new industrialized landscape they saw in the area and, sitting side by side, made many pencil sketches of the bridge and the buildings beneath it. These often formed the basis of finished watercolours, one of which, *Bedlam Furnace, Madeley Dale, Shropshire,* Munn exhibited at the Royal Academy the following year. The view is one looking to the east along the bank of the River Severn and shows the furnaces, smiths' shop, joiners' shop, engine house, casting

house and belching chimneys. The smoke which fills the air comes from the coke hearths situated above the furnaces. Various bits of discarded machinery can be seen in the foreground, which shows a road now known as Waterloo Street.

By the 1830s and 1840s views such as Munn's were mostly out of favour with painters and their public alike, and art and nature were seen to be at great odds with science, technology and their results.

JOHN SELL COTMAN

A far more popular form of landscape painting was that which focused on impressive architectural ruins. An artist who became a specialist in antiquarian drawings was Munn's companion in Coalbrookdale, John Sell Cotman, who travelled widely throughout Britain and in northern France. On a trip to Yorkshire in 1803 Cotman stopped off at Crowland Abbey near Spalding in Lincolnshire. The abbey, founded in 716 to commemorate St Guthlac, was a medieval structure mostly destroyed during the Reformation. Cotman saw in the building, with its massive tower and double rows of traceried windows, the possibility of a haunting Gothic image. His experience of drawing the ruins,

PAUL SANDBY MUNN
*Bedlam Furnace,
Madeley Dale,
Shropshire*
1803 Watercolour
32.5 × 54.8 cm
12¾ × 21½ in

THE CHANGING FACE OF THE COUNTRYSIDE

The famous iron bridge at Coalbrookdale constructed by Abraham Darby between 1774 and 1781

Many painters, including J. M. W. Turner and the Swiss Philip James de Loutherbourg, visited the part of Shropshire on the River Severn which, because of both its novelty and its convenient situation on the route to North Wales, had attracted tourists for many years. The picturesque qualities of the landscape around the gorge at Ironbridge were transformed by the often sublime and romantic industrial buildings, kilns, chimneys and ironworks. These, particularly at night, conjured up an awesome image of power and hellish sublimity.

At this time the town of Coalbrookdale could be admired for its natural beauty as well as its evocation of industrial power and progress. Arthur Young, the author of the very popular *Tours in England and Wales*, wrote,

Colebrook Dale itself is a very romantic spot . . . a winding glen between two immense hills which break into various forms, and all thickly covered with wood, forming the most beautiful sheets of hanging wood . . . too beautiful to be much in unison with that variety of horrors art has spread at the bottom.

The 'horrors', an object of fascination here, soon became hideous reminders of the huge problems caused by industrialization. Unemployment, pollution and the generally degraded conditions of life in the great industrial centres of the Midlands and the North, were unable any longer to support that unique fusion of aesthetics and social and economic optimism which had previously motivated artists and writers.

nothing is heard but "Hounds and Horns, Horns and Hounds, Hounds and Horns".' Cotman went on to describe how, while drawing the west front of the abbey, he was subjected to a great deal of interference and 'was obliged to give one of the ringleaders a sound flogging'.

Somehow or other, he concluded, he was able to finish three sketches 'which are quite sufficient to gain a good report of the place'. He was thrilled by the abbey and told Turner that it was 'delicious . . . I feel my pen incapable of describing it – 'tis so magnificent, 'tis most magnificent. The old part full of sketches, the Door, the window – in short the whole, wonderful.'

The Tate's work is one of the vigorous studies which led to a finished watercolour now in the British Museum. The painting has no clear details and is a marvellous example of a rapidly

JOHN SELL COTMAN
Crowland Abbey
c. 1804 Watercolour
21.6 × 15.9 cm
8½ × 6¼ in

however, shows the kinds of problem an adventurous touring artist might encounter in out-of-the-way places. He wrote to his patron, Dawson Turner of Yarmouth, on 18 August 1804. 'You cannot imagine my disagreeable situation in a paltry Inn full of the worst company I ever heard.' This 'company' probably consisted of the members of an otter hunt who were working their hounds on the River Welland, for Cotman wrote that 'The Inn is now quite full and

produced sketch, made on the spot, recording the intense feelings of the artist before a sublime image. A few cows are roughly indicated by ink outlines around patches of colour in the foreground. Whereas such sketches were made spontaneously and with the minimum of technical fuss, a finished piece would be worked on in the studio with even light and temperature and produced slowly, allowing each area of wash to dry before proceeding with others and adding fine detail.

JOHN CONSTABLE

A few years after this rather hectic visit to Crowland by Cotman, John Constable painted a view of Malvern Hall, near Solihull in Warwickshire, which falls into the category of 'country house painting'. In contrast to Crowland Abbey, Malvern Hall was an important modern building remodelled by (Sir) John Soane from an existing structure. The view taken by Constable of Malvern Hall is across a lake; in it are reflected the trees in the middle distance which frame the classical house. Constable has used, for him, an

atypically smooth surface which is none the less very much in keeping with the great tradition of country house paintings.

With Constable's painting, the emphasis is on presenting the country house as a seemingly natural and timeless part of the landscape. Constable's conservative vision fully endorsed such attitudes, even though paintings such as *Malvern Hall, Warwickshire* are rare in the body of his work.

JAMES WARD

Another painting which shows a building in the landscape is James Ward's *Lake and Tower in De Tabley Park* (1814). Ward is best known for his *Gordale Scar,* an example of the taste for the 'sublime' in art during the Romantic period (see page 133). In quite a different vein, the view of the tower in De Tabley Park shows the Gothic folly surrounded by a lake, built by the Leicester family during the years 1761-1767. Ward explained his idea for the painting in an important letter to Sir John Leicester. It is quite clear from this letter that he envisaged the tower as a

JOHN CONSTABLE
Malvern Hall, Warwickshire
1809 Oil on canvas
51.4 × 76.8 cm
20¼ × 30¼ in

JAMES WARD
*Lake and Tower in De
Tabley Park*
1814 Oil on canvas
94 × 135.9 cm
37 × 53½ in

'COUNTRY HOUSE PAINTING'

The tradition of 'country house painting' goes back to the seventeenth century when poets such as Ben Jonson and Andrew Marvell described the houses, and grounds of great landowners as reflections of aristocratic virtue. The order and beauty emanating from the house into the landscape, both of which were always well tended by happy servants and farm workers, embodied the social and moral excellence of the lord of the land. In the later seventeenth century painters such as the Dutchman Jan Siberechts, produced pictures which made these attitudes visible in carefully detailed panoramas.

The 'Prospect' painting as it became known was in effect a kind of portrait and was a counterpart to the grand portraiture of the ruling classes of Britain painted by Sir Peter Lely and Sir Godfrey Kneller which has shaped our image of the great personalities of the period. Usually the view in a 'Prospect' is an elevated or aerial one allowing maximum detail and asserting the centrality of the house in the landscape. A bird's-eye-view also suited the geometrical layout of the extensive gardens which was in fashion until the change of taste to a more informal style in the 1730s.

'beautiful' rather than 'picturesque' or 'sublime' object, and intended the work to be a classical image in the wake of earlier paintings of the same site by Richard Wilson and Turner. Ward paints a calm, balanced image of a pleasant warm summer evening with placid cattle drinking just on the edge of the lake near some graceful swans. An even light bathes the whole scene in which the tower quietly dominates, echoing perhaps the still and watchful figure of the impressive white bull in the foreground.

In his letter to Sir John Leicester, Ward described the bull as 'Adonis', associated in classical mythology with the sun and thus a fitting counterpart to the swans' role as Venus. The complexities of the painting are best explained by the artist himself:

> *The Tower is the subject . . . it is a
> close sultry day . . . when the air is
> charged with Electric fluid –
> preparatory to a Thunderstorm. A
> gentle breeze is slowly running over
> the surface of the lake which gives it
> the colour by a very imperceptible
> ripple, which increases on the near*

side, by which I am enabled to preserve the comparative still and elegant forms of the Boats etc. near the Building and a more picturesque form in the Boat near the foreground with the cattle, chaining them together by imperceptible degrees – thus one extreme glides into the other without violence.

This extreme care in composition extends to uniting the foliage by the tower with the distant cattle and the bull whose

beauty and vivacity add by contrast to the Repose around and is carried – by the Boat to the speckled Cow whose colours are made to harmonise with it and lead to the more strong coloured Cow . . . – and the swallows independent of the sentiments add as another link to the

chain – leading to the swans whose classic form and hue act as a contrast to and yet assimilate with the tower etc. etc.

Although written in defence of the work to a doubting patron, Ward's letter gives a clear idea of the devices used by artists in the nineteenth century and allows us to appreciate their highly developed 'language' of art.

FARMERS AND LIVESTOCK

More remarkable cattle of the early nineteenth century can be found in the Leicestershire-born Benjamin Marshall's 'portraits' of John Willkinson's short-horned breed, painted in 1816. Wilkinson was a pioneer breeder of this kind of cattle; he lived in Nottingham, whose splendid castle dominates the rather Italianate background in the picture.

BENJAMIN MARSHALL
Portraits of Cattle of the Improved Short-Horned Breed, the Property of J. Wilkinson, Esq, of Lenton, near Nottingham
1816 Oil on canvas
101.6 × 127 cm
40 × 50 in

PETER DE WINT

The great park surrounding the castle, in those days owned by the Duke of Newcastle, was let out as grazing land to local farmers such as Wilkinson. The foreground of the painting is dominated by a majestic bull, a celebrated beast, who went by the name of Alexander, and also three cows and a calf.

As Stubbs had painted horses for proud owners, so Marshall presents the cattle for the admiring gaze of their owner.

There is a faintly comic aspect to the picture in the juxtaposition of the animal portrait group and a strongly classical landscape. All the animals in the work seem just a little surprised to be the object of an artist's attentions, although the little we know about Benjamin Marshall as a man would suggest that he was a bon viveur with an immense sense of humour.

Peter de Wint is perhaps the great landscapist of the Midlands. The 'peasant poet' John Clare, who came from Northamptonshire, summed up many admirers' feelings about De Wint's unpretentious vision when he described the great painter's breathtaking watercolours 'that breathe the living freshness of open air and sunshine'. It was hard luck on John Clare that the socially rather aloof De Wint ignored most of the poet's sincere, well-meaning and very flattering attentions.

Born in Hanley, Stoke-on-Trent, and trained as an engraver and portrait painter in London, De Wint turned to landscape painting in 1806. In the same year he visited Lincoln with his friend, the artist William Hilton, whose sister Harriet he later married. De Wint painted in many parts of England but had a special relationship with

PETER DE WINT
Bridge over a Branch of the Wytham
c. 1812 Watercolour
41.6 × 51.4 cm
16⅜ × 20¼ in

115

Lincoln and the surrounding countryside. His view of a bridge over a branch of the River Wytham in Lincoln is an early watercolour which shows the probable influences of John Varley and John Sell Cotman in its structural clarity. De Wint creates a mood of extreme peace and calm on a hot summer's day, contrasting the laundress fetching water under the bridge with the peasant above leaning on the fence.

Typical of De Wint's style is the very detailed finish given to the weeds and grasses in the foreground of the painting, based on separate studies, and the rich effects in the brickwork similar to those that can be achieved when working with oil paint.

PETER DE WINT

Peter de Wint 1784-1849

Peter de Wint was a very successful watercolourist, fetching up to 50 guineas for a finished work, but failed to sell many oil paintings. His dealer John Vokins was surprised to find, after De Wint's death, that the artist had an attic converted into a gallery full of unsold oils. Nevertheless De Wint's great success as a watercolourist enabled him to keep houses in both London and Lincoln. He was also an important teacher, whose qualities Ruskin described humorously and perceptively in 1840:

He despises all rules of composition, hates Old Masters and humbug ... never was

abroad in his life, never sketches anything but pig-styes and haystacks, and is a thorough-going John Bull of an artist. But, to make amends

for all this, he is a most ardent lover of truth – hardly ever paints except from nature, attends constantly and effectually to colour and tone, and produces sketches of miraculous truth of atmosphere, colour and light....

This is an extremely significant statement, as it anticipates Ruskin's espousal of the Pre-Raphaelites' 'truth to nature' ten years later and also records a major shift in taste away from 'all rules of composition' and 'humbug' which had been associated with eighteenth-century procedures in art.

De Wint's basic imagery, however, is conservative and nostalgic, dominated by cornfields, harvesting and reaping, and finding strong echoes in the work of John Constable. Like Constable, De Wint combined a traditional view of society with a progressive and experimental attitude to art.

His contemporary James Orrock explained how De Wint 'flooded his paper, and drove the running colour in masses deep into it; the lay-in was therefore rich and full in the extreme, and looked like mosaics'.

De Wint used a heavily grained, ivory-tinted Creswick paper which was perfect for creating the mottled highlights typical of his work.

GEORGE ROBERT LEWIS

Farm labourers as the dominant subject in British landscape art are not common, though there are countless rustic-looking figures to be found. George Stubbs painted a number of memorable images of field workers and Constable was concerned in his Stour Valley pictures to document a working landscape (see page 92). George Robert Lewis, a painter of German descent about whom little is known, lived for a while in Hereford where he worked as a drawing master. He painted his view of Hereford and the Malvern Hills in 1815, the year of Napoleon's defeat. The view taken is from Haywood Lodge, a few miles south-west of Hereford, looking east towards Dinedor (or 'Dynedor') Camp which is south-east of Hereford. To the right is the ridge of Marcle Hill. It is a hot summer afternoon and some sturdy harvesters in the foreground are taking a rest, drinking or chatting, while further away on the right of the picture a laden haycart drawn by two horses is being tended to by labourers; other men at work can be seen beyond the trees to the left. Delicacy and a sense of minutiae are evident in the way Lewis paints the trees and the red, white and blue flowers in the foreground. A peculiarity of the painting is the ghostly figure in the

centre whom Lewis seems to have painted over but not entirely obliterated. He appears to be sitting and attracting the attention of the central figure of the main group.

Lewis was a friend of John Linnell, with whom he travelled to Wales in 1813 and whose *Kensington Gravel Pits* has affinities with Lewis's view of the Malvern Hills in its interest in labour. Lewis also made watercolour sketches of west London at about the same time as his Hereford and Border Country landscapes, including an intriguing view of streets in Paddington being cleared for development. Lewis seems to have been intensely involved in landscape painting for about fifteen years and was a member of the Chalon Sketching Society founded in 1808 by Cornelius Varley and William Turner of Oxford to encourage the study of 'Epic and Pastoral Design'. After 1820 he largely abandoned landscape for portrait painting, which was still a more lucrative trade.

GEORGE ROBERT LEWIS
Hereford, Dynedor and the Malvern Hills, from the Haywood Lodge, Harvest Scene, Afternoon
c. 1815 Oil on canvas
41.6 × 59.7 cm
16⅜ × 23½ in

JOHN ROGERS HERBERT

Nearly fifty years after Lewis painted his bluff and muscular farm workers near Hereford, the Catholic artist John Rogers Herbert created an

PETER DE WINT
A Warwickshire Lane
Watercolour and pencil on paper
34.3 × 52.1 cm
13½ × 20½ in
De Wint's works are notoriously difficult to date. It has been suggested that this is a fairly early watercolour on account of its subdued tonality. Typical of De Wint's style is the vigorous and varied application of paint over a preliminary pencil drawing on cartridge paper.

entirely different kind of harvest scene. The title of his painting, *Laborare est Orare*, means 'to labour is to pray', and it shows the Cistercian monks of Mount St Bernards, Charnwood Forest, Leicestershire, at work in the fields below their church and monastery, which had been designed by Augustus Pugin in the 1840s. The church tower in the distance was probably based on Pugin's drawings, as it had not been built when Herbert visited the abbey in July

1861; in fact the tower was not completed until just before the Second World War and is different from Pugin's design.

This is a religious and moral landscape, as its title suggests. Not only is the monks' work shown as the virtuous tending of God's creation but their social concern is indicated by the scene in the right foreground where a monk offers a poor girl a loaf of bread. Herbert presents a unified image of righteousness, charity

JOHN ROGERS HERBERT
Laborare Est Orare
1862 Oil on canvas
97.2 × 175.9 cm
38¼ × 69¼ in

and nature in a faintly dream-like landscape far removed from the squalor of the cities whence the reformatory boys no doubt came. The artist's identification with the monks is made clear by his presence in the foreground, where he is shown drawing. Herbert was typical of a number of artists in the mid-nineteenth century who found a meaning for their art and life by turning to religion. It was a period of considerable religious debate, with many Christians in England demanding a more ritualistic Church of England and some converting to Catholicism. It was in this climate of spiritual inquiry that the Pre-Raphaelites came to great prominence in the 1850s.

JOHN SINGER SARGENT

By the time the American artist John Singer Sargent painted his famous *Carnation, Lily, Lily,*

JOHN SINGER SARGENT
*Carnation, Lily, Lily,
Rose*
1885-6 Oil on canvas
174 × 153.7 cm
68½ × 60½ in

tion for the work which, he told his sister, was a 'fearful difficult subject. Impossible brilliant colours of flowers, and lamps and brightest green lawn background. Paints are not bright enough and then the effect only lasts ten minutes.' The 'effect' Sargent was after was the mauvish light of late summer and early autumn dusks in September and October and he could only proceed for short periods. Every evening, as the light began to fade, the two sisters, Polly and Dorothy, would put on white dresses; lilies, which during the day stood in pots on the ground, were lifted up on to chairs. Props and models were left in readiness while Sargent and the others played tennis until the exact light required began to work its magic. A witness to this evening ritual was the writer Edmund Gosse who recalled that Sargent would take up his particular place,

> at a distance from the canvas, and at
> a certain notation of the light ran
> forward over the lawn with the
> action of a wag-tail, planting at the
> same time rapid dots or paint on the
> picture, and then retiring again only
> with equal suddenness to repeat the
> wag-tail action. All this occupied but
> two or three minutes, the light
> rapidly declining. . . .

The following summer Sargent retrieved the canvas from the barn where it had been stored and continued work, this time at the Millets' new house in Broadway, where the artist decided to add to the variety of flowers in the picture. He found roses and carnations in the Worcestershire countryside and replanted these in the new garden. When the flowers died as autumn approached they were replaced by artificial ones. The frustrations suffered by Sargent in completing the painting were remarked upon by another artist working in the area, Edwin Howland Blashfield. He saw the canvas on a number of mornings and recalled that it had often been scraped down, thus erasing all the previous evening's efforts.

Rose over the summers of 1885 and 1886, the sort of highmindedness in art found in Herbert's painting was on the wane. It had perhaps been absorbed into the Arts and Crafts movement in design, typified by the work of the utopian socialist William Morris.

Sargent's painting shows the impact of French Impressionism; he had studied in Paris before moving to England in 1885 and was friendly with Impressionist painters such as Claude Monet. Following Impressionist principles, Sargent's work was painted out-of-doors in Broadway, Worcestershire, at the two houses of his friends Mr and Mrs F. D. Millet. Frank Millet was an illustrator and had soon gathered around him at Broadway a virtual colony of American artists. Sargent undoubtedly became the 'star' artist and personality at the house, where he also met his great admirer the American novelist Henry James.

The two young girls in the picture, staring into the glowing Chinese lanterns, were the daughters of the illustrator Frederick Barnard who lived nearby. Their golden hair was precisely the hue that Sargent wanted. Sargent sketched them at play many times in prepara-

The trials and tribulations were all worth while, however, as the painting was a huge success when it was shown at the Royal Academy in 1887. The late-Victorian audience adored the beautiful and innocent girls in their oriental-cum-upper-middle-class setting and found Sargent's rather laboured version of Impressionism far more acceptable than the real thing. The painting has an intensity and a poignant beauty about it, in spite of Sargent's own later mocking title for it, 'Darnation, Silly, Silly, Pose!' (The original title came from a popular song of the period.) Where Ruskin and the mid-Victorians, including the Pre-Raphaelites, had tried to describe the minute detail of the natural world, Sargent looked to transitory light effects and a complex surface of pattern and texture. Sargent is said to have derided Ruskin's notion of 'truth to nature' and was once heard to exclaim, 'Ruskin, don't you know – rocks and clouds – silly old thing!'

The profound changes in art in the twentieth century have meant that for many modern painters both Pre-Raphaelite truth-to-nature and Impressionist spontaneity are outmoded reactions to the natural world. New ideas about form and imagery as well as a more pessimistic or even tragic view of man and his environment have led some artists to create a sombre kind of landscape vision which nevertheless has its roots in Romanticism.

Paul Nash is well-known for his war paintings from both world wars. His masterpiece of the Second World War is *Totes Meer (Dead Sea)* painted in 1940 and 1941. It is based on sketches and photographs of a wrecked aircraft dump at Cowley, near Oxford, made by Nash while working as an official war artist. Under an eerie green sky with a waning moon, the mass of tangled metal seems like a sea of icy breakers. Nash's description of the scene to Sir Kenneth Clark in 1941 encapsulates the artist's feelings about this uncanny image: 'You might feel – under certain influences – a moonlight night for instance – this is a vast tide moving across the .ields... And then, no: nothing moves, it is not water or even ice, it is something static and dead... The only moving creature is the white owl flying low over the bodies of the other predatory creatures, raking the shadows for rats and voles.'

PAUL NASH
Totes Meer (Dead Sea)
1940-1 Oil on canvas
101.6 × 152.4 cm
40 × 60 in
Nash seems here to have had in mind the work of the great German Romantic painter Caspar David Friedrich (1774-1840) whose Arctic Shipwreck *(c. 1823-4) shows a ship lost in the midst of thick broken sheets of ice. Whereas Friedrich's landscape is utterly cold and dead, however, Nash's suggests some persistent life and movement.*

THE
NORTH OF ENGLAND

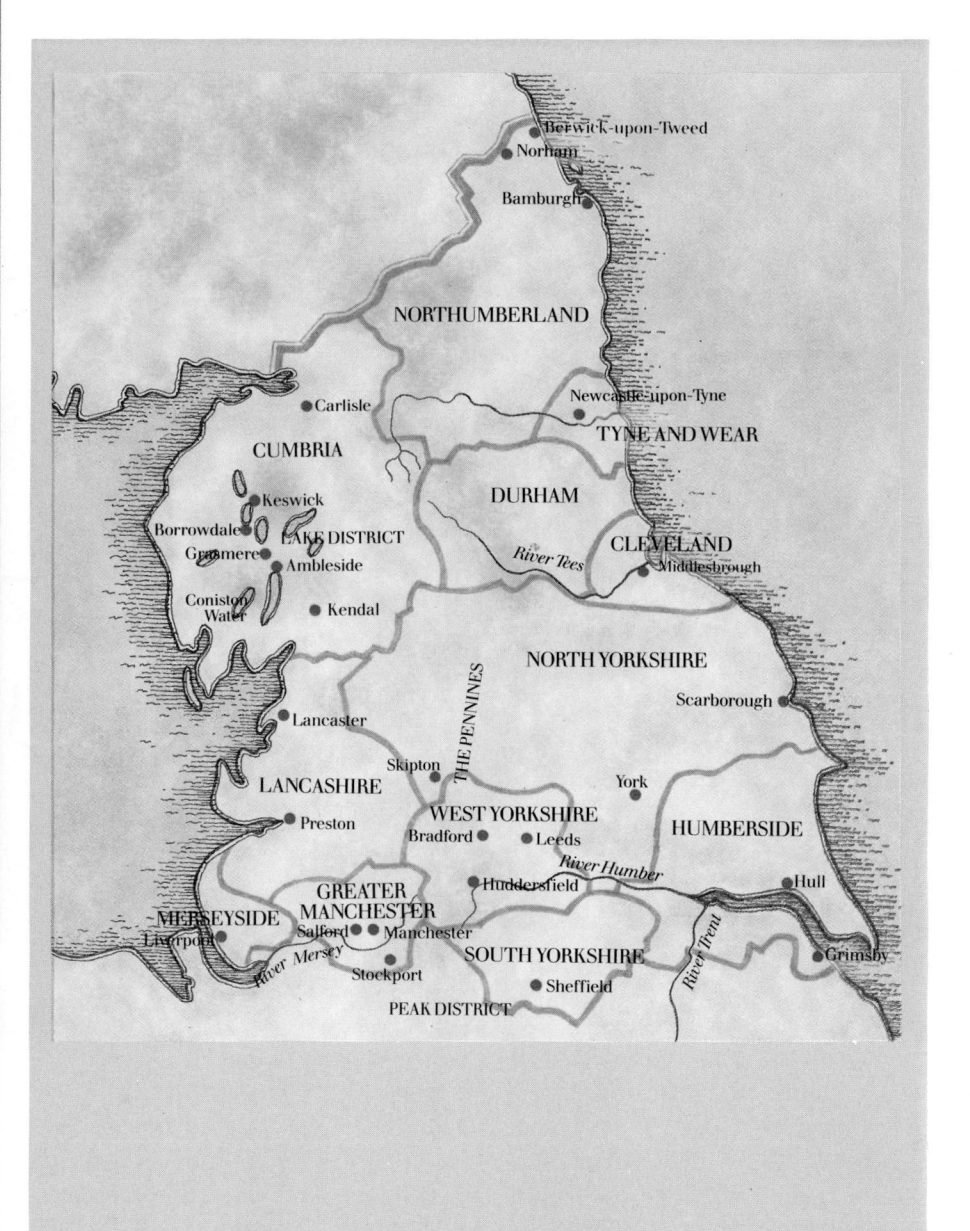

LEFT: The lake district, an area of sublime beauty that is so often associated with the romantic poets, has also captured the imagination of such great painters as J. M. W. Turner and Atkinson Grimshaw

The landscape of northern England is varied not only geologically but also culturally. The great industrial areas – on the Tyne, Wear and Mersey rivers, in the great manufacturing towns, and in the mining centres – have each achieved a unique character which stems as much from their economic activities as from their natural appearance. For all the importance of the human aspects of the landscape, however, relatively few artists over the centuries have chosen to depict it. John Atkinson Grimshaw and L. S. Lowry are the only great geniuses of the industrial scene; most painters have found inspiration in the conventional beauty of the Lake District, the Peak District and Northumberland. This is significant in understanding the way in which received ideas have shaped artists' perceptions of the landscape. The great factories, collieries and ports of the North were considered unsuitable as subjects for painting on two counts: they seemed visually ugly, and they represented the world from which landscape art was meant to be an escape. Today we have a rather different view of such scenery, but in the eighteenth and nineteenth centuries artists, and their public, preferred the aesthetically safer pleasures of mountains, valleys and lakes.

ARTHUR DEVIS

One of the most charming and unexpected views of the North is Arthur Devis's *Breaking-up Day at Dr Clayton's School at Salford* painted between 1738 and 1740.

Dr John Clayton founded St Cyprian's School, better known as Salford Grammar, in 1735, for the sons of wealthy conservative families with Jacobite and High Church sympathies. The school was in deliberate competition with the free-thinking Manchester Grammar School. Tradition has it that Clayton, standing on the left, is shown in this painting listening to some of his pupils recite poetry prior to the start of a school holiday. He holds a scroll on which is visible one of his favourite quotations from the Latin poet Horace's *Exhortation to the young Lollius*, which reads 'Now drink in these words with a pure heart, boy . . .' The school was well-appointed and had been founded with the intention of giving its smart young gentlemen a strict education in the classics and, as can be seen by the globes and scientific apparatus, in modern subjects as well. The open room in which Clayton and some of the boys stand is pure invention, showing a sundial high up on its

cornice with the time standing at four o'clock, signifying the end of the school day. As if to underline the new carefree atmosphere in contrast to the discipline of the recital, a boy sits astride a balustrade and picks honeysuckle, which he throws into a hat held out beneath him. In the meadow below the terrace other boys are skipping, fishing, practising archery, flying a kite and taking a leisurely stroll.

This particular work is an elaborate example of the rococo 'conversation piece' for which Devis is best known and which he practised so successfully in the North-west of England in the mid-eighteenth century.

The background shows a rather idealized view of the Peak District, uninterrupted by the massive, grey industrial developments which were to start later in the century and to be so brilliantly and memorably painted this century by L. S. Lowry, who actually lived for many

JOHN PIPER
Seaton Delaval
1941 Oil on canvas
71.1 × 88.3 cm
28 × 34¾ in
In 1940 John Piper was commissioned to paint watercolours of important architecture under threat for the Recording Britain *project. In 1941 he painted a number of country houses, including Seaton Delaval, Northumberland, a building by Sir John Vanbrugh. The architecture, which had fallen into disrepair in the nineteenth century, provided Piper with an opportunity to develop his 'theatrical sublime' style. The war era is evident in the moody colours and ravaged surface of the painting.*

years in Salford (see page 137).

CHANGING ATTITUDES TO LANDSCAPE

The example of the Lake District offers a vivid insight into changing attitudes to the British landscape over the centuries. In 1685 a remarkable and intrepid young woman called Celia Fiennes embarked on a tour of England and kept a wordy, somewhat breathless journal of her views and feelings. Although greatly impressed with the spectacular waterfalls of the Lake District, she was pleased to leave the mountains and avoided going further north into Cumberland where, she said, 'I should have found more such and they tell me farr worse for height and stonynesse.'

Fiennes was far more interested in towns and in the cultivated landscape and, in these preferences, was merely voicing a generally shared view of her time. 'Wild' nature was a threat to man's livelihood and the impassable fells and rugged hills of the Lake District were a dangerous inconvenience to the civilized traveller. A few years later Daniel Defoe, the journalist and author of *Robinson Crusoe*, wrote his *Tour Through England and Wales;* having visited the towns of Lancashire, he approached the Lake District anticipating an inhospitable land of hidden terrors and inhuman bleakness. He was not disappointed and, as he traversed this barren wilderness, he constantly prayed to reach some arable land and a welcoming town with all its business and gossip.

ARTHUR DEVIS
Breaking-up Day at Dr Clayton's School at Salford
c. 1738-40 Oil on canvas
120.7 × 174.6 cm
47½ × 68¾ in

Today it is surely the opposite view that prevails – namely, that cultivated land is at best tame and attractive and at worst an over-rationalized bore, and that towns are claustrophobic, dirty and dangerous. Climbers and ramblers now head for the open spaces of Cumbria to struggle over the volcanic peaks or stroll in the hills above the great lakes. The beginnings of this change in attitude lie in the mid-eighteenth century, when writers such as Thomas Gray visited the Lakes and began to appreciate their unique and sublime natural beauty. It was a beauty, however, composed and framed in the enthusiast's eye by conventional artistic ideas. The Cumbrian Dr John Brown wrote to Lord Lyttleton in 1753, 'the full perfection of KESWICK consists of three circumstances. Beauty, Horror, and Immensity, united; ... to give you a complete idea of these three perfections ... would require the united powers of Claude, Salvator and Poussin.' By referring to these three great landscape painters of the seventeenth century, Brown was conforming to the contemporary view that nature only became worthy of attention through art. This attitude to the landscape is most closely associated with the category of the 'picturesque', first written about in detail in the 1780s by another Cumbrian, William Gilpin, in his *Observations, Relative Chiefly to Picturesque Beauty*. William Gilpin described landscape as if it were a painting and strongly stressed 'roughness', variety, intricacy and 'brokenness' as the main characteristics of the picturesque view.

By the 1780s there was a full-blown tourist literature on the Lake District, the most popular guides being those written by the Scottish writer Thomas West. He gave detailed instructions on how to reach certain viewpoints, or what he called 'stations', and how to appreciate the scenery from them in an 'aesthetic' fashion.

Not only did West instruct his readers on how to compose the scenery in pictorial terms but he further justified an appreciation of the Lake District by comparing it favourably with the Swiss and Italian Alps.

Gainsborough was an early visitor to the Lakes in the summer of 1783 and his *Landscape with Herdsman and Cows Crossing a Bridge* was one of the results. He told a friend that it would show 'that your Grays and Dr Brownes were tawdry fan-Painters'. As with most of his landscapes, exact representation is here dispensed with in favour of an atmospheric lyrical vision. When working towards such paintings, Gainsborough used sketches made out of doors, his own memory, imagined sketches and small models. His friend William Jackson mentions Gainsborough's use of 'little laymen' for his

THOMAS GAINSBOROUGH
The Bridge
c. 1783 Oil on canvas
40 × 48.3 cm
15¾ × 19 in

FRANCIS TOWNE
A View at Ambleside
1786 Watercolour
15.6 × 47.3 cm
6⅛ × 18⅝ in

PHILIP JAMES DE
LOUTHERBOURG
*Lake Scene in
Cumberland: Evening*
1792 Oil on canvas
42.5 × 60.3 cm
16¾ × 23¾ in

THE APPEAL OF THE LAKES

In the 1790s, when British tourists were unable to visit the Continent because of war with France, the Lakes were positively bristling with 'Lakers', as they were known, paying five shillings a day for a guided tour. Armed with a guide book, sketching pad and a Claude glass which was a black convex device which reflected scenes in miniature, the typical and often rather ridiculous 'Laker' became the object of satire in the 1790s, in plays and in poems such as William Combe's famous *The Tour of Dr. Syntax in Search of the Picturesque*, illustrated by the caricaturist Thomas Rowlandson. The absurd character of Syntax was based on William Gilpin and utters many of his prescriptions on picturesque beauty in the Lake District.

A more serious view of the picturesque and a more accurate understanding of the Lakes in particular became dominant by 1800 and is evident in both painting and poetry. The poet William Wordsworth, a native of Grasmere, went to live in Dove Cottage with his sister Dorothy in 1799, and later wrote his *Guide to the Lakes*, which became a standard work for tourists. He exhorted the visitor to look at the simple and beautiful facts of the scenery rather than view through pictorial conventions.

human figures and cattle, modelled in clay.

The Swiss painter, Philip James de Loutherbourg, visited the Lakes in the same year as his friend Gainsborough, although it is not known if the two men met there. De Loutherbourg was a stage designer who specialized in landscape effects. In 1781 he built his 'Eidophusikon' in London's Drury Lane, where the audience was treated to cunningly staged scenes complete with moving clouds and changing light effects. His *Lake Scene in Cumberland: Evening* (1792) is a classic example of the picturesque view.

SIR GEORGE BEAUMONT AND THE LAKE DISTRICT

The painter and collector Sir George Beaumont was one of the most important artists who travelled in the Lake District. Beaumont was a pupil of Richard Wilson (see pages 142–145); his art is imbued with a strong classical feeling while at the same time showing the influence of the Dutch realist artists of the seventeenth century. The diarist Joseph Farington records Beaumont painting with works by Meindert Hobbema and Peter Paul Rubens in front of him for aesthetic guidance. His *Waterfall at Keswick* is one of a number of *plein air* (open-air) sketches made while staying with the poet Samuel Taylor Coleridge's landlord, William Jackson, in the summer of 1803. Coleridge later told Beaumont that he had burst into tears when he saw this particular work, one of two the artist left behind him after his stay with Jackson.

It will give a lasting interest to the Drawings of the Waterfall, that I first saw it through tears. I was indeed unwell and sadly nervous; and I must not be ashamed to confess . . . that I found a bodily relief in weeping, and yielded to it.

Beaumont and Wordsworth both shared similar views about landscape with their mutual friend and keen correspondent Uvedale Price, whose *Essays on the Picturesque* of 1794 described a new and conservative vision of landscape. Price believed that the aim of the lover of the picturesque should be to appreciate the way in which

SIR GEORGE BEAUMONT
Waterfall at Keswick
1803 Watercolour
31.1 × 27.9 cm
12¼ × 11 in

J. M. W. TURNER
*Morning Amongst the
Coniston Fells,
Cumberland*
1798 Oil on canvas
122.9 × 89.9 cm
48⅜ × 35⅜ in

which Turner had visited during a tour of the
North in 1797 and shows his fascination with
complex effects of light and atmosphere.
Clouds, mountains, fells and waterfalls seem to
dissolve into a misty haze, highlighted by the
golden rays of the early morning sun.

RAMSAY RICHARD REINAGLE

The year after John Constable's largely unsuc-
cessful visit to the Lakes in 1806, Ramsay
Richard Reinagle, a painter who was at first
Constable's friend but is later constantly vilified
in his correspondence, visited the region in the
company of the artist William Havell. Reinagle
was a child prodigy who first exhibited at the
Royal Academy at the age of 13. In 1803 he set up
his own 'Panorama' in London, showing views
of Rome, Florence and Naples, and much of his
work at this time was directed to providing material for these popular entertainments. The
enterprise quickly proved a financial failure,
however, and Reinagle turned his attention to
highly finished landscape drawings, particularly of the Lake District. *Loughrigg Mountain
and River Brathy, Near Ambleside – Sunset*, exhibited at the Society of Painters in Water
Colours in 1808, is an idealized and smoothly
painted view in the style of some artists of the
Bristol School (see pages 12–14) and in marked
contrast to the speedy bravura (boldness) of the
oil sketches he made on location. It is perhaps
typical of what Constable spoke of as Reinagle's
ability to describe nature 'minutely and

things grow slowly and naturally without 'improvement' and how this should be seen as a
virtue in society as well. Price attacked the
builders of grand houses with sweeping lawns
in the Lake District and, like Wordsworth,
bemoaned the eventual transformation of the
area into a vast holiday park for weary escapists
from the city.

J. M. W. Turner, as a young man, made his
living as a topographical artist and painted
many views of Britain in watercolour. The start
of his career coincides with the flowering of interest in the picturesque during the decade
when British tourists were forced to look to
their own country for uplifting scenery. Turner
also exhibited British landscape views in oil at
the Academy, where two superb Lake District
images were displayed in 1798. *Morning
Amongst the Coniston Fells, Cumberland* shows
the famous mountain, the Coniston 'Old Man'

RAMSAY RICHARD
REINAGLE
*Loughrigg Mountain
and River Brathy, Near
Ambleside-Sunset*
1808 Watercolour
51.1 × 71.1 cm
20⅛ × 28 in

cunningly, but with no greatness or breadth'. Certainly, compared with Turner's 'mists and exhalations' it is a very charming but unadventurous illustration.

THE INFLUENCE OF THE PRE-RAPHAELITES

By the 1850s the Lake District was full of wealthy middle-class people seeking retirement and the 'moral power' Wordsworth had discerned in the landscape. John Ruskin, the great art critic and social reformer, had first visited the Lake District at the age of 5 and remembered 'the intense joy, mingled with awe, that I had in looking through the hollows in the mossy roots, over the crag into the dark lake'. Subsequent visits as an adult, culminating in his move to Brantwood on Lake Coniston in 1871, had helped him to define the principles of what he called 'natural composition', as against the artificial rules that had previously dominated man's aesthetic vision.

Ruskin believed the artist should observe nature with a scientific exactitude and paint a meticulously precise image. This led him to champion the young Pre-Raphaelite painters such as Dante Gabriel Rossetti, John Everett Millais and William Holman Hunt in the early 1850s and to become the spokesman for many of their followers. One such follower, early in his career, was the Leeds artist John Atkinson Grimshaw. Probably under the influence of one of Ruskin's protégés, J. W. Inchbold, also from Leeds, he painted a number of Lake District works in the 1860s, one of which, *Bowder Stone, Borrowdale* (*c.* 1865), was only rediscovered as late on as 1983.

The Bowder Stone is a famous natural phenomenon, weighing about 2,000 tons and with a set of steps allowing the tourist to surmount it. Grimshaw's painting is a perfect example of the later Pre-Raphaelite style, with its hallucinatory detail painted in bright colours on a white ground. This technique allows for maximum translucency and brilliance and gives the foreground, all-important to the Pre-Raphaelites and Ruskin, a particularly photographic quality. We know, in fact, that Grimshaw, who was self-taught, used photographs for some of his other Lake District paintings of this particular period, and it seems likely that he did the same for this work too.

Ruskin had approved the use of the daguer-reotype, one of the earliest types of photograph, as a useful memory aid for the artist in his search for a faithful rendering of minute natural detail. He described the new science of photography as one of the very few good things to have come out of 'all the mechanical poison that this terrible nineteenth century has poured upon men'.

Ruskin would have particularly approved of the way in which Grimshaw used photography in relation to his painting, as he made many subtle but important changes in his works and never became the slave of the photographic machine.

THE 'BEAUTIFUL', THE 'PICTURESQUE' AND THE 'SUBLIME'

Images of other parts of northern England during the early nineteenth century tended to be based on picturesque ideas of beauty as much as were those of the Lake District. Turner's exact contemporary, Thomas Girtin, earned a living, like his celebrated friend, by touring Britain and making picturesque water-colour drawings in the 1790s.

Both Turner and Girtin worked in the even-ings as draughtsmen and watercolourists for Dr Thomas Monro of Adelphi Terrace in London, who gained admission for Girtin to the Royal Academy. Girtin was a brilliant student whose tragic early death from consumption in 1802 Turner believed saved his own career from obscurity. Girtin was capable of superb atmos-pheric effects and also of creating a brooding power in his landscapes; his paintings, such as *Bamburgh Castle, Northumberland,* have an in-dividual quality his contemporaries would have

JOHN ATKINSON
GRIMSHAW
*Bowder Stone,
Borrowdale*
c. 1865 Oil on canvas
40.6 × 54 cm
16 × 21¼ in

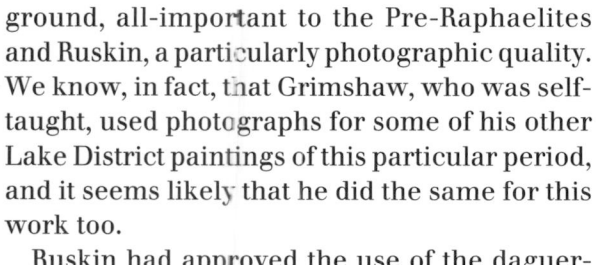

Ward has introduced groups of wild animals peculiar to the country and, among others, his favourite, the bull. These give the desired effects to the enormous cliffs and we doubt whether a more perfect presentation of the VAST in nature, was ever produced on canvas.

In Ward's day the Scar, set in the heart of the northern Pennines, was a day's walk from Settle for the enthusiastic tourist in search of picturesque and sublime views.

Thomas Gray, one of the first writers to commend the splendour of the Lakes, was also an overawed visitor to Gordale Scar in 1769. He subsequently wrote of the 'horror of the place' and described how

from its very base it begins to slope forwards over you in one block and solid mass without any crevice in its surface and overshadows half the area below . . . I stayed there (not without shuddering) a quarter of an hour, and thought my trouble richly paid, for the impression will last for life . . . .

By the early nineteenth century the view was one of the most celebrated in the country. Girtin's teacher Edward Dayes exclaimed, 'Good heavens, what a scene, how awful, how sublime', and it is said that the influential Sir George Beaumont claimed the Scar was so sublime that it could not be painted.

This proved an irresistible challenge to the quarrelsome cockney James Ward. Ward was the most successful animal painter of his day; he was compared during his lifetime with the

described as 'sublime'.

James Ward's massive painting of Gordale Scar (*c.* 1812-14), is one of the great exercises in the 'sublime'. A contemporary review gives a good idea of the subject as well as of its appeal to Ward's audience.

It is at once wonderful as a superior work of art, and wonder-working in its effect on the mind of spectators. It represents a vast dell formed by perpendicular cliffs of limestone strata, at a place called Gordale Scar, near Skipton, in Yorkshire. A chasm in the rocks, down which falls a cascade, enlightens the gloom on a plain at the bottom on which Mr.

THOMAS GIRTIN
Bamburgh Castle, Northumberland
c. 1797-9 Watercolour
54.9 × 45.1 cm
21⅝ × 17¾ in
Girtin's view of the ruins of this Northumbrian castle makes this building appear to grow out of the rock. Painted on warm 'biscuit' colour cartridge paper on which he first drew a quick sketch, Girtin's mottled effects are achieved through a series of pale colour washes laid over one another and augmented with blots and streaks of darker colour, punctuated by touches of white.

THE 'SUBLIME'

Like the Picturesque, the 'Sublime' was a category in art defined during the eighteenth century. It was promoted by Edmund Burke, who published his highly influential *Philosophical Enquiry into the Origin of our Ideas of the Sublime and Beautiful* in 1757. The significance of Burke's ideas, which derived in part from those of the classical writer Longinus, was that they challenged the orthodox view which made the 'beautiful' the highest form of aesthetic emotion.

This overturned an established tradition of thought and represents a major shift in the philosophy of art, opening up many new possibilities for painters. By stressing the emotional aspect of art Burke made the artist's function far more subjective and less constrained by academic rules. Anticipating the mood of the Romantic period, Burke described the Sublime as that which overawed the spectator, made him feel extremely insignificant and

threatened his life. Its typical qualities were obscurity, infinity, vastness and a sense of some unimaginable power. Burke wrote, 'whatever is in any sort terrible or is conversant about terrible objects or operates in a manner analagous to terror is a source of the sublime.' Such feelings of terror could be experienced in nature, and particularly in wild and desolate landscape like that at Gordale Scar in Yorkshire, with its huge rocky cliffs and rolling clouds.

JAMES WARD
A View of Gordale, in the Manor of East Malham in Craven, Yorkshire, the property of Lord Ribblesdale
1812-14 Oil on canvas
332.7 × 421.6 cm
131 × 166 in

LEFT: Gordale Scar, set in the heart of the northern Pennines. In 1811 the idea of capturing this massive landmark on canvas proved irresistible to the cockney artist James Ward

great Dutch painter of cattle, Paulus Potter. He was also a greatly admired and versatile landscape artist and was one of the obvious choices for Lord Ribblesdale when he decided to commission a large painting of the most dramatic part of his estate in 1811. Ward visited Ribblesdale's house, Gisburn Park, in August that year and made studies and sketches of Gordale Scar. Over the next three years Ward worked towards his final enormous canvas. He greatly exaggerated the scale of the Scar and made other adjustments to the real site, which show his

country's mortal struggle against Napoleon.

TURNER IN YORKSHIRE AND NORTHUMBERLAND

While Ward was painting this truly megalomaniac picture, one of his keenest rivals in the depiction of the sublime, Turner, was trying his hand at an altogether different kind of image: *Frosty Morning,* exhibited in 1813. This was highly praised by Constable's great friend and patron, Archdeacon Fisher, who told Constable

J. M. W. TURNER
Frosty Morning
1813 Oil on canvas
113.7 × 174.6 cm
44¾ × 68¾ in

J. M. W. TURNER
Snow Storm: Hannibal and his Army Crossing the Alps
1812 Oil on canvas
146 × 237.5 cm
57½ × 93½ in

main concern was to overwhelm the viewer with an unprecedentedly sublime and prehistoric image. It could be said Ward had taken great liberties in bringing together a variety of viewpoints, none of which by itself could give us the stormy scene as Ward has painted it. Certainly the bull and the other animals were out of place, as Lord Ribblesdale kept them in his park at Gisburn, well away from the rocky wilds of the Scar. As we have found in many other paintings of this period, there may also be a symbolic reference to the war with France which was being waged at this time. The bull, which Burke had described as 'definitively sublime', was also a symbol of England and represents the ancient strength of the native breed protecting his family from attack. In this way Ward brings together the tourist's sense of the natural sublime with the more alarming fear induced by his

that it was the only painting better than his at the Academy that year. He went on to add, 'But you need not repine at this decision of mine: you are a great man like Buonaparte, and are only beaten by a frost.' This painting is not really typical of Turner's work but none the less shows why his contemporaries considered him to be virtually unassailable in matters of landscape. As a reviewer wrote when the painting was shown at Turner's gallery over twenty years later in 1835, 'the frosty ground, the naked trees, the cold, dead, white sky, and the pale, weak, yellow gleam of sunlight, that scarcely relieves the cheerless desolation, or lessens the cold of the air, are imitated with the most delicate truth.' The painting is said to show Turner's own old bay horse. Turner said he sketched the scene while travelling in Yorkshire by stagecoach, which he has put in the distance.

Turner may well have been making a visit on this occasion to one of his greatest patrons, Walter Fawkes, who lived at Farnley Hall, near Leeds, where Turner had a studio in which he worked most years between 1810 and the time of Fawkes's death in 1825. Turner loved the countryside in Wharfedale, which seems to have been the inspiration for one of his most sublime historical landscapes, *Snow Storm: Hannibal and his Army Crossing the Alps*, exhibited at the Academy in 1812, while Ward was in the middle of work on *'Gordale Scar'*. Fawkes's son, Hawksworth, remembered how

> *one stormy day at Farnley Turner
> called to me loudly from the
> doorway 'Hawkey! Hawkey! come
> here! look at this thunderstorm. Isn't
> it grand? Isn't it sublime?' All this
> time he was making notes of its form
> and colour on the back of a letter. . . .
> He was absorbed; he was entranced.
> There was the storm rolling and
> shafting out its lightning over the
> Yorkshire hills. Presently the storm
> passed and he finished. 'There!
> Hawkey!' said he. 'In two years you
> will see this again, and call it
> Hannibal Crossing the Alps.*

If this story is true, and there seems no reason to doubt it, there could hardly be a finer example of the way in which the Romantic painter transformed a real landscape into an historical and poetic sublime image.

In this case Yorkshire becomes the Alps, which the legendary Carthaginian general Hannibal crossed in 218 B.C. Typically Turner shows Hannibal as an imperceptible figure on

ABOVE: Wharfedale in Leeds, the inspiration for J. M. W. Turner's sublime, historical landscape: Snow Storm: Hannibal and his Army Crossing the Alps *1812*

a barely visible elephant totally overwhelmed by the vast overarching stormy sky. A comparison with Ward's painting shows Turner to have been an incomparably greater painter of powerful light and atmospheric effects. In contrast with Turner's painting, *Gordale Scar*, for all its immensity, seems stagey and unreal.

The verses from Turner's unending manuscript poem 'Fallacies of Hope' warns of the decadence and decline that will be the Carthaginian leader's eventual fate as he is seduced by the pleasures of the Mediterranean:

In vain each pass, ensanguin'd deep
 with dead,
Or rocky fragments, wide destruction
 roll'd,
Still on Campania's fertile plains –
 he thought,
But the loud breeze sob'd, 'Capua's
 joys beware!'

For Turner's audience this moral message was an expected ingredient of a grand historical landscape and would also be seen as having considerable relevance to their own historical situation. Such imagery taught that the past acts as a warning to the present. All empires rise and then decline after 'luxury' has set in. Turner

was personally obsessed with this particular theme, as can be seen in many of his great exhibited paintings. '*Snow Storm*', just like most of his paintings until the 1830s, was received rapturously, the critics went wild, enthusing about its 'effect of magic' and hailing Turner as 'this Prospero of the graphic arts' who 'is in the highest rank of landscape painters'.

Turner's great popularity, as is well known, declined in the last twenty years of his life as he began to experiment with paint in his search for ever more ethereal and beautiful impressions of light and colour. Much of this experimentation took the form of watercolour studies, known as 'colour beginnings', which seem almost abstract in their insubstantial washes of colour, and often unfinished canvases, never exhibited, which attempt to create similar effects in the far more difficult medium of oil paint. A miraculous work such as *Norham Castle, Sunrise*, which could never have been exhibited, would have been considered by Turner to be a true expression of his perception of this great medieval pile on the River Tweed.

Turner had first visited Norham, in Northumberland on the Scottish border, during his tour of the North Country in 1797. The following year he made a large and accurate watercolour

J. M. W. TURNER
Norham Castle, Sunrise
c. 1845 Oil on canvas
90.8 × 121.9 cm
35¾ × 48 in

JOHN ATKINSON
GRIMSHAW
*Liverpool Quay by
Moonlight*
1887 Oil on canvas
61 × 91.4 cm
24 × 36 in

*smelling dye, and vast piles of
buildings full of windows where
there was a rattling and a trembling
all day long, and where the piston
of the steam engine worked
monstrously, up and down, like the
head of an elephant in melancholy
madness.*

This was the world Ruskin wished to escape by moving to Brantwood, where only a deep involvement with nature could redeem the 'mechanical poison' of the century. Most artists and their audience concurred with Ruskin in denying this new and terrible world a place in art. Indeed, art had become without doubt the only means of transcending or evading the poverty, grime and ugliness which was the price of economic growth.

It is therefore interesting to find Grimshaw, who had earlier painted jewel-like landscapes of the Lake District, turning later in his career to moon-lit scenes of the docks and harbours of great ports. In these works, such as *Liverpool Quay by Moonlight* (1887), there is still a concern for photographic exactitude but the scene is veiled in an eerie gas-lit darkness which gives the hard facts of the urban world a mysterious magic. Grimshaw had a studio in Chelsea in the mid-1880s and is said to have been a friend of the great American painter James Abbott McNeill Whistler. Like Whistler, Grimshaw loved the way in which nights in the city offered a shimmering poetry unattainable elsewhere.

The year Grimshaw painted Liverpool Quay, L.S. Lowry was born in Manchester. He was to become the most famous painter of the northern industrial scene, even though he spent his life working as a clerk for a property company and living in the unglamorous surroundings of Salford. Lowry learned to paint and draw at evening classes at local art schools and led a lonely, reclusive existence, living at home with his parents for many years. He was a pupil, at the Manchester Municipal School of Art, of the interesting but little-known French artist Adolphe Valette, who specialized in impressionistic urban scenes populated with isolated figures. Lowry was considered an eccentric character by those who met him, wearing awkward, untidy clothes as he went rent-collecting and every now and then stopping in the street to make sketches of people, buildings, chimneys and so on. His typical subjects were the towns and their inhabitants, which surrounded him and he called his paintings 'documents'.

Unlike many of his artistic contemporaries in

of Norham Castle from sketches made out of doors. When he returned to the subject in his old age Turner used the same viewpoint, from the English bank of the Tweed, and seems to have based his general composition on his youthful work. The result, however, is radically different. Now the castle becomes an eerie, ghostly blue presence surrounded by water, in which the rays of the hazy sun dissolve in limpid stillness. Hills are faintly visible in the distance and evanescent cattle lap the water in the foreground.

INDUSTRIAL LANDSCAPES

For many people over the last hundred years and more, the North of England has been identified with a new, industrialized landscape. Charles Dickens's description of 'Coketown' in *Hard Times* evokes the classic northern industrial scene:

*It was a town of machinery and tall
chimneys, out of which interminable
serpents of smoke trailed themselves
for ever and ever, and never got
uncoiled. It had a black canal in it,
and a river that ran purple with ill-*

THE ENVIRONMENT OF L. S. LOWRY

The grim poetry of L. S. Lowry's environment was revealed to him by chance in 1916 in Pendlebury when he noticed the end of the day routine at the Acme Spinning Company's mill:

The mill was turning out hundreds of little pinched black figures, heads bent down . . . hurrying across the asphalt, along the mean streets with the inexplicable derelict gaps in the rows of houses, past the telegraph poles, homeward to high tea

L. S. Lowry 1887-1976

or pubwards, away from the mill and without a backward glance.

In the 1930s this scenery was further overshadowed by the appalling effects of the Great Depression and this allowed Lowry to make his figures seem even more oppressed by their environment. Lowry was obsessed by crowds and the strange mixture of uniformity and individuality which can be perceived in them. These are lonely, stick-like robots who move from factory to park or terraced slum under belching chimneys, prison-like warehouses and an ever-present grey sky.

L. S. LOWRY
Dwelling, Ordsall Lane, Salford
1927 Oil on panel
43.2 × 53.3 cm
17 × 21 in

L. S. LOWRY
The Pond
1950 Oil on canvas
114.3 × 152.4 cm
45 × 60 in

the 1930s, Lowry did not seek to make overt political comments in his paintings. He maintained a detached, even alienated view of what he saw and painted it in a simple and naïve style. His work was 'discovered' by a London art dealer in the 1930s and he was given a one-man show in the capital in 1939, which proved very successful and led to the Tate Gallery's purchase of *Dwelling, Ordsall Lane, Salford* (1927) the same year. From this point on, Lowry was a national celebrity and one of the most popular painters ever in Britain. In spite of this public attention and increasing wealth, he stayed in the North and was extremely proud never to have travelled overseas, bought a car or had a telephone installed.

Lowry's most famous and complex paintings he called 'dreamscapes'. By this he meant that they were of no identifiable view but rather made up of fragments taken from sketches and transformed into detailed panoramas evoking the look and atmosphere of the places he knew. He began by painting his canvas white, often twice, allowing it to dry and then painting over this with a very restricted number of colours. Other than white and black, he used yellow ochre, vermilion and Prussian blue. These were mixed to produce a surprisingly wide range of subtle hues and tones. The invented quality of

Lowry's paintings is underlined by his method of starting with some building or other in the centre of the composition and then adding further details of buildings and streets bit by bit until he had a townscape; he then filled it with figures who cast no shadows and seem trapped not only in space but also in time.

Lowry's spontaneous, piecemeal approach was the subject of a letter he wrote to the Tate Gallery when it purchased *The Pond* in 1950. He had no idea when he started it, he said, how the painting would turn out.

The result was one of his most intricate and imposing works, with its extraordinary array of chimneys, factories, warehouses and terraces surrounding the huge pond where workers find a few hours' pleasure in their rowing boats under the eternal dirty white, smog-laden sky. Even this huge open space in the heart of an industrial town had an airlessness about it. It is an image almost of some kind of reformed hell where the only deadly punishments are routine and captivity.

As can also be seen in his magnificent *Industrial Landscape* painted a few years later, Lowry characteristically finds room for his beloved Stockport Viaduct, one of the most impressive pieces of industrial architecture in the region.

WALES

On the map:

Holyhead · Anglesey · Llandudno · Rhyl

Denbigh

Caernarfon · Capel Curig · **CLWYD**

Llanberis · Betws-y-Coed · Wrexham

Snowdon · Conwy

GWYNEDD

Arenig Fawr

Harlech

Dolgellau · *River Dee*

Cader Idris

Penegoes · MOUNTAINS

POWYS

Aberystwth

CAMBRIAN

Cardigan · *River Teifi* · *River Wye* · *River Severn*

Fishguard · *River Ystwyth*

St Davids · **DYFED** · *River Usk*

St Bride's Bay · *River Tâf* · **BRECON BEACONS** · Abergavenny

Milford Haven · Llanelly · Monmouth

Pembroke · **WEST GLAMORGAN** · **GWENT**

Swansea · **MID GLAMORGAN** · Chepstow

Caerphilly

SOUTH GLAMORGAN · Cardiff

LEFT: The towering peak of Cader Idris, a great symbol of the mythical past and timeless natural power of Wales. These qualities were captured perfectly in Richard Wilson's work Llyn-y-cau, Cader Idris, *exhibited in 1774 (page 145)*

J. M. W. TURNER
Caernarfon Castle
c. 1798 Oil on panel
15.2 × 23.2 cm
6 × 9⅛ in
Painted on a tour in the summer of 1798 this sketch is on a small pine panel prepared with a red ground. Turner seems to have been influenced by the painter Sawrey Gilpin in the use of red, which can be seen through the paint surface.

Wales began to attract the attention of painters in the late eighteenth century, the period when it became popular with tourists. Wales was a symbol of a lost Celtic past and its people, customs and landscapes appealed to travellers on account of their exotic 'difference'. Here was a landscape, it seemed, untouched by the scourge of progress and industrialization, a haven for jaded town dwellers weary of their 'civilized' lives.

Following Richard Wilson, painters such as Julius Caesar Ibbetson, Thomas Girtin, J. M. W. Turner, Paul Sandby and John Sell Cotman flocked to North Wales, in particular, to record the towering mountains of Snowdon and Cader Idris, the romantic castles of Harlech and Dolbarden, and the great rivers and lakes. In the mid-nineteenth century David Cox stressed the bleak but enduring power of Wales, painting a landscape in which the people are part of a natural process from which there is no escape but within which a grim, even beautiful, dignity is possible. This kind of oppressive beauty is even evident in the deserted landscapes of the twentieth-century painter Graham Sutherland, who made Pembrokeshire his second home.

RICHARD WILSON
Richard Wilson is usually regarded as Wales's

JOSEF HERMAN
*Pregnant Woman with
Friend* 1945
Pastel and pencil over
watercolour on paper
64.8 × 89.5 cm
25½ × 35¼ in
*The subjects of this painting
are a pregnant woman and
older friend standing on the
'Teddy Bear Bridge' at
Ystradgynlais in the
Swansea Valley in South
Wales, where the artist had
moved in 1944. He shows
the women as massive
presences in a powerful,
brooding landscape.*

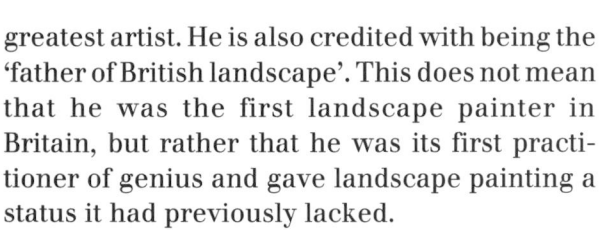

greatest artist. He is also credited with being the 'father of British landscape'. This does not mean that he was the first landscape painter in Britain, but rather that he was its first practitioner of genius and gave landscape painting a status it had previously lacked.

Wilson was born in 1713 or 1714 in Penegoes, Powys, where his father was the local rector. He received a good classical education before moving to London at the age of 15 to study painting with the portrait painter Thomas Wright. In the early 1750s he travelled in Italy, arriving in Rome in 1752. While in Rome Wilson made many sketches and drawings of the surrounding countryside, the Campagna, which served him in good stead for the rest of his career. The painter and diarist Joseph Farington wrote that it was this early study of the Roman landscape which 'formed his taste, and from the various matter which he found in those celebrated places he composed many pictures and stored his mind with classical ideas which enabled him to form those beautiful compositions'.

The key word here is 'classical': Wilson had studied Rome and the Campagna because of their classical connotations. He painted works, on his return to England, which followed the classical style of Claude Lorraine, the great seventeenth-century French painter who had worked in Rome. Claude used a recognizable set of compositional and painterly devices which Wilson's contemporaries would have called 'beautiful'.

The typical Claudian view is framed by trees in the foreground; these establish the depth of the picture, which recedes in an orderly succession of planes, often linked by a path or river, leading the eye to the horizon. Everything in the painting is intended to induce a sense of tranquil order. This style was the approved mode for landscape in the eighteenth century and Wilson's paintings were hugely popular with his classically educated, aristocratic patrons who made Rome the focal point of their Grand Tours. The Grand Tour was embarked upon by most young aristocrats, men of learning and artists as a kind of finishing school after their formal studies. Rome was always the final destination, being the most important city in the classical world.

Although Wilson's first great successes in the 1750s were with classical landscapes obviously based on famous Italian sites such as Tivoli, Lake Nemi, Hadrian's Villa and so on, he began a little later on to adapt the Claudian format to British landscape views.

When it came to painting views of his native Wales, Wilson adopted both classical and non-

THE INFLUENCE OF THE CLAUDIAN STYLE

The tendency to adopt the classical Claudian style of composition in art (named after the renowned seventeenth century French painter Claude Lorraine) was paralleled in the landscape gardening of the time: the vast gardens built by the Hoare family at Stourhead in Wiltshire were designed in this classical manner, with their framed views, temples and lakes. Thus parts of Britain were imaginatively recreated in the image of Italy, confirming the ruling class's sense of being the

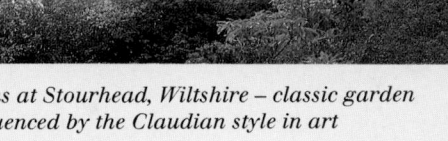

The gardens at Stourhead, Wiltshire – classic garden design influenced by the Claudian style in art

true inheritors of the classical tradition. At Stourhead Henry Hoare II wanted his house and landscape to reflect this tradition 'which distinguishes only the Gentleman from the vulgar'. In the house hung works by Claude, Poussin and Gaspar Dughet while his gardens were living pictures and a walk through them was a journey through antiquity. Hoare also believed his 'paths of Paradise' were 'the fruits of industry and application to business and shows what great things may be done by it, the envy of the indolent who have no claim to temples, grottos, bridges, rocks, exotic pines and ice in summer.'

RICHARD WILSON
*View near the
Loggerheads, Denbigh*
c. 1765-70 Oil on canvas
41.9 × 52.1 cm
16½ × 20½ in

classical formats. His *View near the Loggerheads, Denbigh,* painted some time in the late 1760s, is certainly Claudian. It is, in fact, a highly personal image; it takes its viewpoint from outside the grounds of Colomendy Hall, near Llanferres, which was the property of Wilson's cousin, Catherine Jones, and looks north-west across the River Alun which runs between the cliffs of Pen-y-Carreg Wen. The reference to the 'Loggerheads' in the title is to an inn of that name, which is out of sight in a dip in the middle distance. According to tradition, Wilson, who drank a great deal, was very fond of this inn and painted the sign for it in part-payment of his debts to the landlord. The sign is now kept in a glass case on the outside of the pub and shows the profiles of two men with the inscription 'We three Loggerheads', the third party being the viewer. Wilson spent his last, poverty-stricken years of illness at Colomendy Hall and was buried in the churchyard at Mold.

Wilson's *Llyn-y-Cau, Cader Idris,* is a rather different and more complex kind of image painted during the same period. The view here is from the slopes of Mynydd Moel looking down to the volcanic lake Llyn-y-Cau, which is near the top of Cader Idris in North Wales. The dramatic sharp peak above the lake, Craig-y-Cau, dips and then rises to the main peak on the right. Behind Craig-y-Cau, to the left, is the Dysynni Valley and in the far distance is Cardigan Bay. In many respects this painting also conforms to the grand classical style, in its conventionalized foreground with its carefully arranged boulders and the slightly elevated viewpoint which puts the spectator, as it were, in control of the scene. The actual site is far less coherent than Wilson has shown, Craig-y-Cau in particular forming a much less regular shape. What might have been a rather awesome and threatening sight is given an order which allows us to contemplate it with a certain amount of detached pleasure which the aristocratic aesthetic requires. In spite of this, however, the subject matter transforms the painting into an image which in many respects works against its broad classical structure.

In Wilson's painting we have a wonderful, lasting document of the earliest developments of tourism in Wales, with its diminutive figures

RICHARD WILSON
Llyn-y-Cau, Cader Idris
Exhibited 1774
Oil on canvas
51.1 × 73 cm
20⅛ × 28¾ in

carefully examining the stunning lake or scanning the expansive, breathtaking views with a telescope.

Perhaps one of the figures in Wilson's painting is the quaint Ralph Edwards, an eccentric local guide, whose handbills advertised him as,

> *CONDUCTOR TO, and over the most tremendous mountain CADER IDRIS, to the stupendous cataracts of CAIN and MAWDDACH, and to the enchanting cascades of DOL-Y-MELYMLLYN, with all the beautiful romantic scenery, GUIDE-GENERAL and MAGNIFICENT EXPOUNDER of all the natural and artificial curiosities of North Wales.*

THE GROWTH OF TOURISM IN WALES

As was the case with the 'discovery' of the Lake District by writers and painters, the 'discovery' of Wales, and especially North Wales, took place during the second half of the eighteenth century. The traveller Rev. J. Milles felt much the same about Wales in 1735 as Daniel Defoe did about Cumberland in the 1720s: it was bleak, barren and thoroughly uncomfortable for a civilized and urbane city dweller. By 1777, however, this attitude had altered very dramatically, and the travel writer Joseph Cradock describes Wales's great beauty thus: 'the gay attire of fertile vales and woods, the plainer dress of mountains, cataracts and craggy precipices, more beautiful by change, and more pleasing by variety'.

In North Wales these qualities were augmented by what one anonymous tourist called an 'angry grandeur' which, unlike the Lakes, had not been disfigured by the commercialization which usually attends the growth of tourism. The traveller in North Wales could still feel like an explorer, alone in the wilds of an uncharted region and free to experience the natural world unimpeded by too many reminders of his cultural origins. The native Welsh were always an added attraction, with their exotic dress,

The picturesque dress and countenance of the Welsh women we passed on the road delighted me; their clean caps, blue flannel cloaks and black hats added to their independent way of riding behind each other, bespoke a hardy useful race who were really the help-mates, not the encumbrances of man,

wrote the extremely patrician-sounding writer Mrs West.

These admirable qualities were regarded by tourists as the product of the hardy surroundings and historical background of the Welsh. Descendants of the Ancient Britons who had been forced west by successive waves of invaders, the Welsh held a great fascination for the romantically inclined visitors who came to Wales. Thomas Gray's celebrated poem 'The Bard', published in 1757, the year Wilson returned from Italy, was one of the most important works of the 'Celtic revival'. It deals with the tradition of Edward I's massacre of the Welsh bards, the poets who preserved their native language. The last bard, standing on a rock above the River Conway, curses the Norman invaders and then hurls himself into the torrent. This immensely popular poem brought together a whole range of its audience's passions and interests. The Welsh, with their ancient language, beautiful harp music and simple lifestyle, were the very image of humans unspoilt by the excesses of progress and civilization. This was the age of the Swiss philosopher Jean Jacques Rousseau and his widely influential notion of the 'noble savage', when intellectuals felt the need to discover the origins and primitive essence of man.

Cader Idris was a great symbol of Wales's mythical past and its timeless natural power. From its peak, the sublime views conjured up literary images for the educated tourist keen to embellish his experience with poetic allusions.

When I stood upon the edge of this precipice and looked into the frightful abyss of clouds, it put me in mind of the chaos, or void space of darkness, so finely described in

ANTHONY VANDYKE COPLEY FIELDING
Cader Idris from the Barmouth Sands
1810 Watercolour
21.3 × 65.4 cm
8⅜ × 25¾ in
This very wide panoramic view shows the great mountain, so popular with tourists, under a great burst of sunlight. In the foreground on the left trees with expressively shaped branches seem to rear up before the scene like monstrous horses. Fielding, who came from Halifax, first visited Wales in 1808.

*Milton, where the fallen archangel
stood at the gates of hell, pondering
the scene before him and viewing
with horror the profound expanse of
silence and eternal night.*

Thus does J. Hucks, describing Cader Idris in his *Pedestrian Tour Through North Wales* of 1795, express that delight in the 'sublime', discussed in greater detail on pages 131–32.

WILLIAM WILLIAMS

A fine example of a highly literary Welsh landscape is William Williams's *Thunderstorm with the Death of Amelia* (1784).

Little is known about Williams, who was active between 1758 and 1797. The landscape itself, which shows Penmaenmawr Valley in Caernarfonshire, is rather fantastical, with its split pine tree and grotesque fallen branches in the foreground, steep outcrop and burning castle in the middle distance, and the spectacular peak of Snowdon beyond the lake.

The subject is taken from the most popular landscape poem of the eighteenth century, James Thomson's *The Seasons*. The scene is of an episode from 'Summer', with Celadon holding the body of his lover Amelia, who has been struck dead by the lightning flash which has also split the tree and set fire to the castle.

Thomson's poetry was much used by artists during this particular period and the lines Williams illustrates are,

> *From his void embrace*
> *Mysterious heaven! that moment, to*
> *   the ground,*
> *A blackened corse was struck the*
> *   beauteous maid.*
> *But who can paint the lover, as he*
> *   stood,*
> *Pierced by severe amazement, hating*
> *   life,*
> *Speechless, and fixed in all the death*
> *   of woe.*

What is notable is the extent to which profound human emotions find their natural setting in a wild and sublime landscape where the human figure is alone and vulnerable. Previously, as in

WILLIAM WILLIAMS
*Thunderstorm with the
Death of Amelia*
1784 Oil on canvas
63.5 × 101.9 cm
25 × 40⅛ in

*RIGHT: Penmaenmawr
valley in Caernarfonshire,
scene of William Williams's
highly literary landscape*
Thunderstorm with the
Death of Amelia *1784*

the work of William Hogarth for instance, dramatic scenes tend to be mainly set in towns and houses and have a social meaning. In the kind of painting Williams has made, not only do love and death find intense significance in the landscape, but their power seems to lend the natural world a human quality. The shapes of the tree and branches and also the rocky promontory beyond have an exaggerated and theatrical aspect which is intended to express the overwhelming feelings involved.

The painting is roughly divided into dark and light halves. The lightning strikes in the dark section, where Celadon's turbulent feelings are shown in his gesture of despair. The eventual peace of death and acceptance of it are suggested in the light half, where Snowdon, 'dissolving, instant yields his wintry load'. Such devices are typical of Romantic art and can be found later, for instance, in John Constable's moving *Hadleigh Castle* of 1828-9 (see page 94), where the motion is transferred far more directly into the paint surface and the literary background is correspondingly less important.

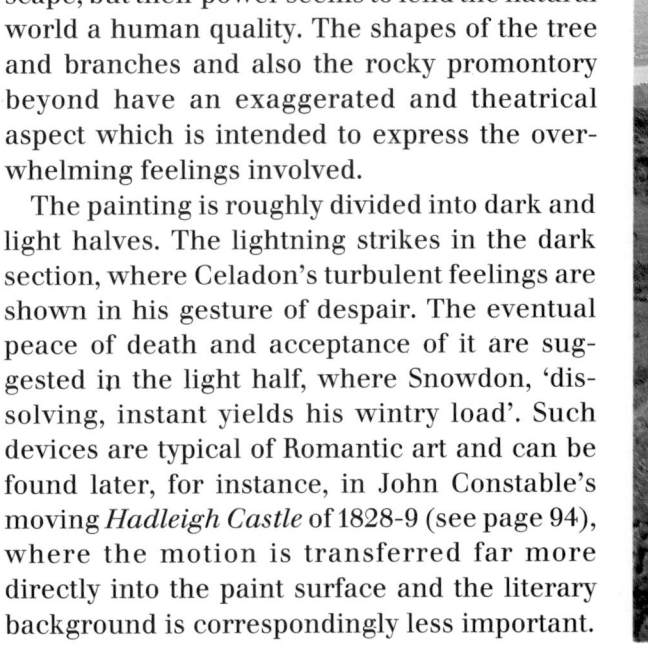

CORNELIUS VARLEY

Cornelius Varley is typical of the landscape painters of this time, who not only painted detailed watercolours but also began to show greater interest in a more spontaneous kind of painting in which the atmosphere and the 'sentiment of the subject' became of over-riding importance. Varley, who was never really a professional painter, was one of the young artists who congregated at Dr Thomas Monro's house in London's Adelphi Terrace and went on sketching trips with him to Surrey. He travelled to Wales on a number of occasions, sometimes in the company of his brother John, an artist and occultist, and, on a lone trip in 1805, made some remarkable studies which show his very strong scientific interests. Under the direction of his uncle, Samuel Varley, Cornelius learned to make lenses for microscopes and telescopes and later in his life was the inventor of a 'graphic telescope' for use by artists. He also took a keen interest in meteorology and wrote of his 1805 trip to Wales,

> I travelled to North Wales quite
> alone, for the whole season was so
> rainy that in most places I was the
> only traveller. This apparent solitude
> mid clouds & mountains left me more
> at large 'To hold converse with
> Natures Charms & view her stores
> untold'. Having been familiar with

SIR GEORGE BEAUMONT

Sir George Beaumont 1753-1827

In the late eighteenth century Sir George Beaumont, the powerful patron, connoisseur and painter, travelled frequently in both the Wye Valley and North Wales. Between 1799 and 1806 he leased Benarth, a now semi-derelict house above the River Conway, which became a favourite summer haunt for guests such as Thomas Girtin and John Sell Cotman. During this period Turner, Ibbetson, Sandby and Cornelius Varley all visited North Wales which, as a result of Britain's wars with France, had become, like the Lake District, an alternative to the Alps and other mountainous regions on the Continent. The Welsh landscape allowed all these painters the chance to experiment in 'beautiful', 'sublime' and 'picturesque' images, the three main categories of landscape art.

JOHN SELL COTMAN
Ruins and Houses, North Wales
c. 1800-2 Watercolour
25.1 × 35.6 cm
9⅞ × 14 in
This was presumably painted after one of Cotman's tours in Wales in 1800 and 1802. The 'wooly' watercolour technique used to depict irregular cottages, gothic ruins and rustic figures makes this a fine example of the 'picturesque' style.

CORNELIUS VARLEY
Evening at Llanberis
1805 Watercolour
20 × 23.8 cm
7⅞ × 9⅜ in

*the known Electrical experiments I
was better prepared & more at
liberty to observe and understand
what I saw.*

Varley wrote detailed descriptions of atmospheric conditions near Snowdon, for example describing how he 'saw and understood the gradual progress from a cloudless morning to universal rain here was a silent invisable [*sic*] flow of electricity to the mountains'. This scientific approach lies behind the simple and beautiful watercolour wash, *Evening at Llanberis*.

SAMUEL PALMER

Samuel Palmer, best known for his landscape painting in Shoreham, Kent, travelled by steamer from London to North Wales in the summer of 1835 in the company of the painters Edward Calvert and Henry Walter. Palmer found particular inspiration in the waterfalls, which were one of the great tourist attractions of Wales. William Mavor, the author of *The British Tourist 1798-1810,* recorded a visit to Wales in 1805 and wrote with great enthusiasm of the sublime effects of waterfalls,

*Every circumstance that enters into
the composition of this scene is
calculated to inspire fear and horror.
Where the eye cannot fathom depths,
and noise is heard without being
able to trace its cause, fancy is no
longer under the control of
judgement, and it creates terrors of
its own.*

Palmer's delicate, prismatic painting, *The Waterfalls, Pistil Mawddach, North Wales*, probably painted after his return from Wales, shows a shift in interest from that of Mavor, Palmer looking instead for a light-filled, almost fairy-like image. Rather than present sensations of 'fear and horror' Palmer offers instead a shining vision of nature in its benign aspect.

There is a sense here, suggested by the small rainbow above the water, of a divine light at the heart of all things. For Palmer this light was the artist's quest both within himself and without. In a letter from North Wales the following year, Palmer asserted in a memorable passage,

Blessed thoughts & visions haunt the stillness & twilight of the soul; & one of the great arts of life is the manufacturing of this stillness. The middle station of life, where more is demanded to be done than there are hands enough quietly to do, almost forbids it; & the rooms of our houses are so crowded together that we less

enjoy life than listen to the noise of its machinery. It is like living in a great Mill where no one can hear himself speak. So I think the fewer wheels the better – but what matters how I think – whom am mad on this subject? – Mad I mean to be till I get more light, & wherever I find it will turn to it like the sunflower.

This is one of the great statements of faith in nature and a rejection of the industrialized urban world with its ceaseless activity and din.

The waterfall at Pistil Mawddach becomes a divine machine, whose action and noise are a blessing of perfection and tranquility. Palmer ignores the crashing terror which so awed his predecessors and finds instead an escape from the chaos of the city and modernity. Palmer's son claimed that this painting, which anticipates Pre-Raphaelite art by fifteen years,

SAMUEL PALMER
The Waterfalls, Pistil Mawddach, North Wales
1835-6 Oil on canvas
40.6 × 26 cm
16 × 10¼ in

DAVID COX
A Welsh Funeral, Bettws-y-Coed
c. 1845-50 Oil on paper
54 × 74.9 cm
21¼ × 29½ in

contained his father's 'whole heart'.

DAVID COX

One of the artists most closely identified with Wales is David Cox, who was born in Birmingham in 1783. Cox trained at first as a miniaturist and then as a theatrical scene-painter. When he moved to London in 1804 he took painting lessons with John Varley (see page 109) and made two trips to Wales. In 1814 or 1815, having been appointed as a drawing master at a girls' school, Cox moved to a cottage in Hereford. From here he made some trips to Wales, including a visit to make illustrations for Thomas Roscoe's *Wanderings and Excursions in North Wales* in 1836, the year of Samuel Palmer's second trip to the area. Cox's most important visits to Wales, however, took place between 1844 and 1856, after his return to Birmingham; poor health made it preferable for him to make the short trip to the small village of Bettws-y-Coed rather than go further afield.

One of Cox's most famous paintings of this period is *A Welsh Funeral, Bettws-y-Coed*, now in Birmingham City Art Gallery. The Tate's work of the same title, which shows the same church as the Birmingham picture, and a number of similar figures, is painted in oil on paper. The funeral was that of a young girl relative of the proprietor of the 'Royal Oak' inn in Bettws-y-Coed; Cox frequently stayed there on his visits to the village, which is situated at the junction of three rivers – the Conway, the Lledr and the Llugwy. The ceremony, as is customary in Wales, took place in the evening and Cox has managed to capture the melancholy light catching the bell tower of the church behind the yew trees. The huddled figures walk slowly together towards the church under the mountain and cloudy sky and seem to take part in some natural process as if they are elements of the landscape. The mood of the painting is one of bleak resignation. Life ends in the grave and although Cox was a Christian, his faith is a solemn and unfussy one that may seem gloomy and even doubting. It certainly has none of the glowing sense of divine presence to be found in Samuel Palmer's work.

Cox's view of things may even be said to have a modern air about it, which may partly account for the persistent though mistaken claim that Cox is a forerunner of the French Impressionists. There is certainly some resemblance in his *Rhyl Sands* to the work of the French painter Eugène Boudin, who also painted beach scenes such as this with high skies and isolated groups of figures. Contemporaries remarked of these works that they had a simple honesty about them and yet managed to transcend the banality of a holiday photograph,

> *It is fairywork indeed: and yet all*
> *this is no more than a rugged stony*
> *beach, whereon promenade some*
> *people dressed in forgotten fashions;*
> *a long greyish dun stretch of yeasty*
> *sand; and overhead the nations of*
> *the clouds careering on,*

wrote a critic in 1859 of the larger painting of Rhyl, now in Birmingham City Art Gallery, which Cox made on the same trip in 1854. The Tate's version is sketchily painted in a light palette which, while it is unusual for British landscape art of this period, is by no means 'impressionist'. It is of interest that Cox, who had formerly been a watercolourist, was only beginning to work in oils when this painting was produced, having received some instruction in technique from his friend W. J. Müller.

THE PRE-RAPHAELITES

A Pre-Raphaelite Welsh scene was painted by the obscure artist Ebenezer Downard in 1860. This shows a young peasant girl walking down a path at Capel Curig, near Snowdon, followed by a sheep. Downard shows the same kind of fascination for the detail of the immediate foreground that can be found in much landscape art of the 1850s and 1860s. Scrupulous attention is given to botanical and geological accuracy while, in contrast to earlier views, the distance

DAVID COX
Rhyl Sands
c. 1854 Oil on canvas
45.4 × 63 cm
17¾ × 25 in

EBENEZER DOWNARD
*A Mountain Path at
Capel Curig, Wales*
1860 Oil on canvas
35.2 × 50.2 cm
13⅞ × 19¾ in

is of far less importance and the many spectacular views available in the region are virtually ignored.

JAMES DICKSON INNES AND AUGUSTUS JOHN

James Dickson Innes, who was born in Llanelly in 1887, painted some of the finest Welsh landscapes of the twentieth century while staying near Arenig in the summers of 1910, 1911 and 1912. In 1910 Innes stayed at the foot of the stark mountain, Arenig Fawr, in the village inn at Rhyd-y-fen. The following year he persuaded his fellow Welshman Augustus John to join him on a painting expedition around Arenig and the two men rented a cottage near the village of Nant-ddu. John, who had been searching for some time for a suitable landscape to paint, was thrilled by the mountain and surrounding

JAMES DICKSON INNES
Arenig, North Wales
1913 Oil on panel
85.7 × 113.7 cm
33¾ × 44¾ in

AUGUSTUS JOHN
Llyn Treweryn
1912 Oil on panel
31.8 × 40.6 cm
12½ × 16 in

scenery and wrote to his second wife Dorelia that it was 'the most wonderful place I've seen'.

Innes had gone to the Slade School of Art on a scholarship in 1905 and his early *plein-air* (open-air) landscapes show the influence of Wilson Steer, who had at that time been painting Welsh landscapes in and around Chepstow on the River Wye. After a trip to the South of France in 1908 with his friend John Fothergill, Innes began to use brighter colour and his brushwork became more expressionistic. (Expressionism was a movement in art that began in Germany in the early years of the twentieth century. The concept of Expressionism involves the effect of the artist's emotional state on the subject he or she is painting.)

Innes, who suffered from this time on with the tuberculosis which was to eventually kill him in 1914, had a Bohemian appearance and lifestyle which thoroughly recommended him to Augustus John. Both John and Innes drank heavily yet, in spite of their wild antics together, managed to produce some remarkable landscapes painted on wood panels in the open air. John was struck by Innes's passionate response to the Welsh landscape and remembered that at this time 'Innes's activity was prodigious; he rarely returned of an evening without a couple

of panels completed. These were, it is true, rapidly done, but usually meant long rambles over the moors in search of the magical moment.' Both men used broad strokes of flat colour which capture the scene before them and probably show an interest in the Fauvist work of the French painters Henri Matisse and André Derain.

The differences between the work of the two Welsh artists, however, are marked. Innes's landscape seems on occasion to tremble with volcanic power and emotional turmoil, while John, in his view of the small lake, *Llyn Treweryn*, for instance, paints a more classical and tranquil world. Innes also seems more adventurous in his use of abstract effects typical of Japanese prints and in his raw sense of colour. John believed that much of the power in Innes's work came from a desire to escape his illness. 'This it was that hastened his steps across the moor and lent his brush a greater swiftness and decision as he set down in a single sitting view after jewelled view of the delectable mountains he loved. . .' The intensity of these works is all the more impressive when it is remembered that, until his visits to Arenig, Innes was primarily a watercolourist and he had little experience of oil paint. Even allowing for some guidance by John, the Arenig landscapes are remarkable for their technical skill and vigour.

GRAHAM SUTHERLAND

It was in 1934 that I first visited Pembrokeshire. I was visiting a country, a part of which, at least, spoke a foreign tongue, and it certainly seemed very foreign to me, though sufficiently accessible for me to feel that I could claim it as my own!

Thus wrote the painter Graham Sutherland in 1942 to the editor of *Horizon* magazine.

Sutherland was born in London in 1903, and, after training to be an engineer, studied art at Goldsmiths' College in the early 1920s.

After a period spent designing ceramics, fabrics, travel posters and the like, Sutherland took up painting seriously following his trip to Pembrokeshire in 1934. He made annual summer visits to this rarely painted countryside until the Second World War. His own descriptions of the meanings of Pembroke for him are the best way into Sutherland's art and imagination. The two areas Sutherland explored in greatest depth were either side of St Bride's Bay. On the northern arm of the bay, around St David's, the landscape is very varied, with valleys which,

> *possess a bud-like intricacy of form and contain streams, often of indescribable beauty, which run to the sea. The astonishing fertility of these valleys and the complexity of the roads running through them is a delight to the eye. The roads form strong and mysterious arabesques as they rise in terraces, in sight, hidden, turning and splitting as they finally disappear into the sky. To see a solitary human figure descending such a road at the solemn moment of sunset is to realise the enveloping quality of the earth, which can create*

THE STYLE OF GRAHAM SUTHERLAND

The great influence on Graham Sutherland's early work was the art of Samuel Palmer and in particular Palmer's pastoral etchings. In Sutherland's own etchings of the 1920s a richly textured surface reveals woods and lanes in which trees take on near-human forms, anticipating his later paintings. The natural world is given a dramatic, sometimes sinister quality, full of unexpected forms and forces. Like Paul Nash Sutherland invents a landscape without human

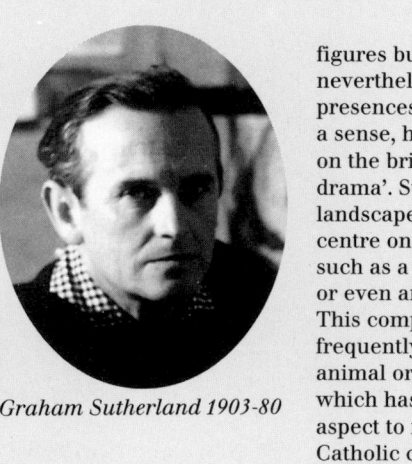

Graham Sutherland 1903-80

figures but which nevertheless reveals human presences, leaving one with a sense, he wrote, 'of being on the brink of some drama'. Sutherland's landscape paintings often centre on a natural form such as a fallen tree, a root or even an animal's skull. This complex shape frequently evokes an animal or human vitality which has a tragic, tortured aspect to it. Sutherland, a Catholic convert, painted crucifixions later in his career which seem to develop from such imagery.

GRAHAM SUTHERLAND
Black Landscape
1939-40 Oil on canvas
81.9 × 132.1 cm
32¼ × 52 in

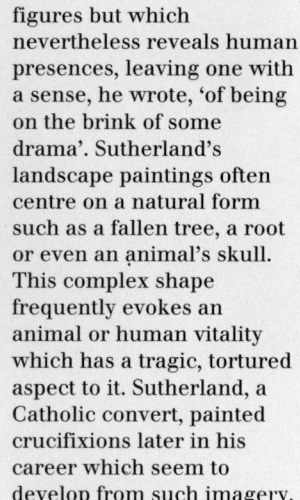

and compression, and do not rely upon illusion.

One of Sutherland's most celebrated paintings is the *Entrance to a Lane* of 1939. This is based on a view of a lane leading up from the west side of Sandy Haven, which lies on the southern arm of St Bride's Bay, along the coast from Milford Haven. This area had a different atmosphere and significance for Sutherland from that around St David's.

Entrance to a Lane was painted from drawings made in July 1939 and again Sutherland creates an enclosed set of forms. In this case a tunnel-like space, with a hidden distant opening, evokes a sense of mystery and anticipation. Flat areas of colour, mostly lush greens, form planes defining a spiralling space which are placed next to thickly encrusted areas of black denoting foreground branches and buds.

Since his discovery of Palmer, Sutherland had searched for his own landscape of the spirit and he found it in the remote strangeness of Pembrokeshire. John Constable said of the Stour Valley that it made him a painter; similarily it was Wales that made Sutherland a painter.

... a mysterious space limit – a womb-like enclosure – which gives the human form an extraordinary focus and significance.

Sutherland's *Black Landscape* (1939-40), painted from a watercolour study made in 1937, shows this twilight landscape and is based on a view near Porthclais, probably of Clegyr-Boia, a rocky outcrop. Sutherland has used a very limited range of colours, contrasting the dominant black with grey and pink, thus creating a mysterious mood which, typically, is rather disquieting. Sutherland stressed that he found it impossible to make realistic finished images from this landscape.

Sutherland would walk through the countryside, occasionally making small sketches, but mostly allowing it to flow through him. The results are paintings which are indeed, as he says, 'paraphrases'. Sutherland's landscape images often have the quality of being self-contained objects in which all the parts, be they mountains, rocks, trees or whatever, are concentrated into dense essences of the scene. Sutherland wrote that Pembrokeshire made him realize that 'landscape was not necessarily scenic, but that its parts have an individual figurative detachment'. His painting continues the Romantic tradition of the early nineteenth century but modifies it by using thoroughly modern techniques which emphasize structure

LEFT: St Bride's Bay, an area that had a special atmosphere and significance for Graham Sutherland

GRAHAM SUTHERLAND
Entrance to a Lane
1939 Oil on canvas
61 × 50.8 cm
24 × 20 in

SCOTLAND

LEFT: The Cairngorms in Winter. In the nineteenth century Scotland was viewed as a romantic land of haunted castles and proud stags. Of the many writers and artists of the time who were instrumental in promulgating this view, Sir Edwin Landseer was amongst the most famous. Loch Avon and the Cairngorms c. 1833 (page 166) captured the popular contemporary viewpoint perfectly

The conventional view of Scotland as the land of kilted Highlanders, remote haunted castles and proud stags is partly a Victorian invention. The writings of a number of authors including Sir Walter Scott, the popularity of the country with Queen Victoria and the evocative paintings of Sir Edwin Landseer were significant factors in the construction of this somewhat romantic view of Scotland.

More so than Wales, with which it shares certain broad similarities of landscape and culture, Scotland became, in a sense, a victim of its own success as a land of fantasy for outsiders. This dream has obscured, for non-Scots, the country's remarkable artistic and intellectual achievements and the real and varied beauties of its scenery. Scotland has been fortunate in producing a succession of talents in the visual arts, however, who have embodied this beauty in their art. From the classical poise of Jacob More to the dour realism of E. A. Walton, Scottish landscape painting has shown a country rich in meaning and scenic beauty.

JACOB MORE

Jacob More was considered by Sir Joshua Reynolds, the portrait painter and President of the Royal Academy, to be 'the finest painter of air since Claude' – referring to Claude Lorraine, the seventeenth-century French landscape painter. Many others, during his lifetime, considered More to be one of the greatest landscape artists in Europe, yet after his death in Italy in 1793 his work was largely forgotten. A

CHARLES COOPER
HENDERSON
*Sportsmen in Scottish
Shooting Dress Driving
to the Moors*
c. 1845 Oil on canvas
33 × 61.3 cm
13 × 24⅛ in
*Four friends dressed in
plaids, tam-o'shanters and
Glengarry bonnets race
through the Moors on a
cart laden with rifles, game
bags, a flask and hamper.
Henderson's works in this
genre were made popular
as aquatint engravings in
the 1840s.*

similar fate befell the great Welsh painter Richard Wilson (see pages 142–145); his reputation did revive in due course of time, however, whereas Jacob More is still relatively little known today.

More was apprenticed to the Edinburgh landscape painter Robert Norie in 1764 and then to the neo-classical artist Alexander Runciman, who introduced him to the circle of the celebrated Cape Club in Edinburgh. He earned his reputation initially as a scenery painter for the Edinburgh New Theatre and by the early 1770s was successfully exhibiting landscapes at the Society of Artists in London.

His most important works of this period were pictures in a series known as *Falls of Clyde*, showing the three great waterfalls on the River Clyde at Bonnington Linn, Corra Linn and Stonebyres Linn ('linn' meaning pool). The Stonebyres painting shows the influence of the French landscape painter Claude Vernet, bringing to a Scottish scene the structure of a classical landscape. More's palette is dominated by cool greys and greens as he builds up an imposing sequence of solid forms and creates stunning effects of air, water and billows of cloudy spray.

Like Wilson in Wales, More painted a local

THOMAS HEARNE
Edinburgh from Arthur's Seat
1778 Watercolour
35.6 × 50.8 cm
14 × 20 in
The artist is concerned here to depict the buildings of the city in some considerable detail, although the grandeur of the setting is not lost on him. Hearne was highly regarded during his lifetime and exerted an influence on the young Turner.

JACOB MORE
Falls of Clyde:
Stonebyres
c. 1771-3 Oil on canvas
80.3 × 100.6 cm
31⅝ × 39⅝ in

landscape with strong historical and mythical meanings. In the case of the *Falls of Clyde* the historical associations are with the military campaign of Sir William Wallace, the Scottish resistance leader who was ultimately captured and executed in London in 1305. These associations helped to make the Falls one of Scotland's first great natural national monuments. These historical resonances, along with the magnificent appearance of the Falls themselves, gave them all the qualities necessary to become one of the great picturesque tourist attractions of the eighteenth century.

It could be said that, More's painting brings together the three main types of landscape art which may be noted in the second half of the eighteenth century: the 'picturesque', the 'beautiful' and the 'sublime'. It also accords with the image of the Falls to be found in con-

temporary literature. In particular James Thomson, whose long landscape poem *The Seasons* had such an important impact on More and other painters of his generation, described Corra Linn in 'Summer'. Such literary references perhaps also help to explain the classical figures in the painting, which lend it a self-consciously grand and generalizing air, emphasizing light, shade and unified composition rather than detail and local effects.

PATRICK NASMYTH

Patrick Nasmyth was the son of the celebrated landscape painter Alexander Nasmyth, who taught him painting from an early age. He suffered from deafness in his teens, as well as receiving a crippling injury to his right hand in an accident while on a sketching tour near Edinburgh with his father. As a result of this mishap he had to learn to draw with his left hand. In 1810 Nasmyth moved to London, where he spent the rest of his fairly short life. Most of his paintings are of English sites with picturesque cottages, trees and ponds forming composite views which are not always accurate representations of the original scene. The presiding influences on his work are those of the seventeenth-century Dutch painters Meindert Hobbema and Jacob van Ruysdael.

Nasmyth's interest in the naturalist tradition led him to undertake a great deal of precise study from nature and he took a particular delight in depicting trees, plants and foliage. Like John Constable he also paid special attention to the sky, observing different light effects and cloud patterns with a meteorologist's eye.

These qualities can be seen in Nasmyth's *Falls of the Tummel*, which shows a foreground figure fishing for salmon in the linn at the foot of the cascade which lies about 3 miles (5 kms) north of Pitlochry in Perthshire.

This is a spot in the Highlands of considerable beauty visited by Queen Victoria in 1844, and surrounded by oak, sycamore, fir, spruce and larch trees. Like most of Nasmyth's work, this was probably painted from drawings made a number of years earlier. His approach tends to play down the romantic possibilities offered by the view and instead presents a straightforward and realistic scene, in keeping with the artist's particular preference for the style of the Dutch painters.

SIR EDWIN LANDSEER

Sir Edwin Landseer is best known for his brilliant animal paintings, which range in their subject matter from the domestic and senti-

PATRICK NASMYTH
Falls of the Tummel
1816 Oil on panel
16.5 × 20.3 cm
6½ × 8 in

LEFT: Glenfeshie in the Cairngorms – one of the places Sir Edwin Landseer visited during his Highland tour in 1833

SIR EDWIN LANDSEER
Loch Avon and the Cairngorms
c. 1833
Oil on Panel
35.2 × 44.5 cm
13⅞ × 17½ in

mental to the wild and disturbing. Many of these works include dramatic landscapes but Landseer is rarely considered to be a landscape painter. He did, however, produce more than a hundred small landscape sketches; many of these are views of Scotland, which he first visited in 1824 when he travelled to Abbotsford to meet Sir Walter Scott.

Landseer seems to have been most interested in the wild and solitary areas of the Highlands and rarely included animals or human figures in these sketches. His favourite views were those of the beautiful Glenfeshie where he stayed with the Duchess of Bedford in rough huts she had built as retreats. Lord Ossulton described an expedition undertaken by the Duchess and her party from Glenfeshie to Loch Avon in the Cairngorms in September 1833. Ossulton recalls that the women slept in a tent overnight while the men slept in a cave above the loch. Landseer, who was on this trip, painted an oil sketch in which the tent, fire, horses and figures are all quite clearly visible. His *Loch Avon and the Cairngorms* was probably also painted on this outing and shows the Shelter Stone Cross seen over the loch. The deep blue lake is surrounded by bare mountains under an ominous bank of dark clouds and Landseer paints with a direct, flat brushwork which gives the scene a simple, unaffected grandeur. A deep shadow falling over the left half of the water increases the effect of changing, threatening weather.

SIR WALTER SCOTT AND JOHN THOMSON

Scotland's appeal to the tourist in the Romantic period was given an enormous boost by the popular success of Walter Scott's novels. One of Scott's close friends was John Thomson, the minister of the kirk at Duddingston near Arthur's Seat on the outskirts of Edinburgh. While studying theology at Edinburgh, Thomson had tuition in painting from Alexander Nasmyth (see page 165) and also came under the influence of the portraitist Henry Raeburn. Thomson exhibited his landscape paintings regularly and made handsome sums from their sale, but nevertheless maintained an amateur status so as not to upset his parishioners. Both Scott and Thomson believed in the importance of feeling and association in the description of landscape, whether literary or painted, and quoted one another's work in their respective media. Scott had helped to change contemporary taste in landscape from the conventions of the eighteenth-century picturesque to a new Romantic freedom – the bare, the wild and the desolate were now endowed with meaning and emotion. Ever since the publication in 1810 of Scott's poem 'The Lady of the Lake', more and more travellers sought out the unexplored splendours of the Highlands. Roads built by General Wade in the 1720s and 1730s were later followed by the great civil engineer Thomas Telford's often superbly landscaped routes. This dramatic discovery of Scotland's beauties and their historical meanings led to nature painters such as Thomson being accorded the highest prestige and accolade.

Loch Katrine, the breathtaking setting for Sir Walter Scott's poem The Lady of the Lake

J. M. W. TURNER IN SCOTLAND

Sir Walter Scott was Master of Ceremonies for the visit of George IV to Edinburgh in 1822, the first state visit to Scotland of a British monarch since the time of Charles II. The romantic nove-

J. M. W. TURNER
Edinburgh Castle: March of the Highlanders
Engraved 1836
Watercolour
86 × 14 cm
3⅜ × 5½ in

list's Tory loyalism led him to cover the city and most of its inhabitants in tartan in an orgy of pageantry which became known as 'the tartan fit'. One of the many artists who visited Edinburgh for this great event was J. M. W. Turner, who was in the process of illustrating Scott's *Provincial Antiquities and Picturesque Scenery of Scotland* and was fascinated by the country. During his visit of 1818 Turner had in fact met John Thomson the clergyman-painter, who admired his work greatly, and the two men became firm friends. Turner was excited by the chance to record an historically momentous event in a series of paintings commemorating the royal progress. Although this series was not realized, Turner did make many in situ (on-the-spot) sketches, as well as a few oil paintings and watercolours. One of the watercolours, *Edinburgh Castle: March of the Highlanders*, was later used to illustrate a book about Scott's

'Waverley' novels. It is based on the procession to Calton Hill associated with the laying of the foundation stone of the National Monument to Scots soldiers who fell in the Napoleonic Wars, which took place during the King's visit. The Mound is shown as a shimmering, fairy-like vision dominating the city; in the foreground ranks of Highlanders march up the hill.

JOHN EVERETT MILLAIS

The great Pre-Raphaelite painter John Everett Millais painted a work in Scotland which he later said was his favourite among his own pictures. *The Vale of Rest* (1858-9) was inspired by the artist's descent of a hill by Loch Awe, from Inveraray, while on his honeymoon with his wife Effie in 1855. Millais was told by his coachman that the ruins of a monastery could be found on one of the islands on the loch and he

JOHN EVERETT MILLAIS
The Vale of Rest
1858-9 Oil on canvas
102.9 × 172.7 cm
40½ × 68 in

JAMES CLARKE HOOK
Home With the Tide
1880 Oil on canvas
88.9 × 139.7 cm
35 × 55 in

and Effie went into a kind of reverie about what life was like in Scotland before the Reformation occurred.

One evening in October 1858 Millais, greatly impressed with a sunset he had witnessed, began the work, taking the wall of the garden at Effie's family home, Bowerswell in Perth, as the background. The beautiful sunsets lasted for a few evenings, allowing him quickly to paint their effect. Meanwhile he continued to paint the old wall, the tall oak and poplar trees behind it, and the terrace and shrubs in the garden. The gravestones are based on those at Kinnoul's old churchyard in Perth and were painted in bitterly cold weather in the company of the sexton, who also obliged by digging a grave for Millais to paint.

The theme of *The Vale of Rest* is mortality. The nun on the left digs a grave so positioned as almost to 'place' the viewer in it. Her companion wears a rosary with a skull and a cross on it and looks sadly out towards us as if to convey her sorrow for our eventual death. In the background a bell in a small tower sounds the Angelus, while above it an ominously coffin-shaped cloud floats behind the trees. In Scotland such a cloud is a traditional harbinger of death. In her description of the work Effie Millais wrote that she and her husband imagined to themselves 'the beauty of the picturesque features of the Roman Catholic religion'. This perfectly expresses the peculiar mixture of nostalgia, aesthetics and uncertain spiritual

feeling typical of the mid-nineteenth-century imagination. The landscape portrayed, based on the observation of actual places and objects, was transformed into a stage where these particular Victorian fantasies are acted out.

JAMES CLARKE HOOK

The later nineteenth century saw developments in the depiction of Scotland that have parallels with those taking place in England and indeed in Europe as a whole. Under the impact of Realism and Impressionism artists sought subject matter with a greater contemporary relevance and a new means with which to convey their vision. An interest in the real lives of people within the landscape led many painters to work and sometimes to live in remote areas where their art could flourish untainted by the sophistication and pretensions of life in the big city. At the same time that artists discovered places such as Staithes, Walberswick, St Ives and Newlyn in England, so Scotland's fishing villages and other as yet unspoilt areas came to prominence.

An English artist who found inspiration in the coastal life of Scotland was James Clarke Hook who early in his career was given great encouragement by Constable. Hook's *Home with the Tide* was painted at Findochty, Banffshire and shows, in the foreground, a woman with her baby, relieved at her husband's return after a fishing trip. Unlike Frank Bramley's *A Hope-*

WILLIAM MCTAGGART
The Emigrants
1883-9 Oil on canvas
94.6 × 141 cm
37¼ × 55½ in

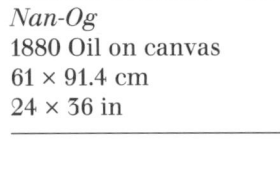

WILLIAM MCTAGGART
Summer Sundown – Tir-Nan-Og
1880 Oil on canvas
61 × 91.4 cm
24 × 36 in

E. A. WALTON
Berwickshire Field Workers
1886 Oil on canvas
91.1 × 61.3 cm
35⅞ × 24⅛ in

less Dawn, set in Newlyn, Cornwall (see page 18–19), this is a story with a happy ending. The scene, which shows the hills of Caithness in the distance, is accurate in its landscape and human detail, but is painted broadly and creates light effects which show some interest in the colour of the French Impressionists.

WILLIAM MCTAGGART

William McTaggart was certainly one of the most original Scottish painters of the nineteenth century. He was born in Argyll, on the Mull of Kintyre, on a small farm near Campbeltown run by his Gaelic-speaking father. His parents were strict Presbyterians who forbade him on moral and economic grounds to draw or paint. After a short apprenticeship to an apothecary, however, McTaggart ignored his parents' wishes and, in 1853, enrolled at art school in Edinburgh where the director of life classes was the famous painter Robert Scott Lauder. Lauder's influence was important for McTaggart, especially in his enthusiasm for broken, spontaneous brushwork using strong colours. By the mid-1870s, having earned success painting in a Pre-Raphaelite manner, McTaggart had developed a unique style which had many affinities to French Impressionism. His *plein-air* landscapes (painted in the open air) led the painter John MacWhirter to tell McTaggart in 1877 that he was justifiably 'the best painter of

open-air in Great Britain'.

From 1876 McTaggart spent every summer near Machrihanish, Kintyre, where he painted many Atlantic seascapes in his by now familiar loose, impressionist style. McTaggart's technique is certain proof of his sheer pleasure in the free handling of paint and of a remarkable feeling for open space and the atmosphere of a particular place.

Although McTaggart often left his coastal scenes empty, or nearly empty, of people, he painted a number of works which dealt with the theme of emigration. The period in which he worked saw the age of the Highland Clearances, when many people, including one of the artist's sisters, left the west of Scotland for Australia, Canada or the United States. *The Emigrants* is one of a series of so-called 'Blue paintings', dominated by that colour, and took a number of years to complete. McTaggart painted the landscape at Carradale, a small fishing port on Kilbrannan Sound, in 1883, and finished the work with the boats and figures by about 1889. Women and children on the shore watch as fishing boats ferry emigrants and their belongings out to a ship anchored in the distance. The image, which verges on the sentimental, shows a poignant understanding of the effect of the Clearances on Scotland and its landscape. A whole area was being depopulated, its character changing beyond recall after hundreds of years of stable existence.

THE GLASGOW BOYS

A group of artists who would have found a great deal in common with McTaggart were those who became known in the 1880s as the 'Glasgow Boys'.

In the late nineteenth century Glasgow, for so long under the shadow of Edinburgh in most cultural matters, experienced a great burst of creative activity. In the visual arts this included the steady growth of the Art Nouveau movement centred around the world-famous architect and designer Charles Rennie Mackintosh, and the appearance of a number of important and enlightened collectors of contemporary art such as Sir William Burrell. The young painters of the Glasgow School included Joseph Crawhall,

MCTAGGART AND IMPRESSIONISM

William McTaggart 1835-1910

The great Scottish nineteenth-century artist William McTaggart, for all his freely expressive brushwork and light airy effects, seems not to have known of the work of Monet and the Impressionists when he forged his personal style. He is said once to have asked a younger painter, 'What is this Impressionism they are all talking about?' The reply came, 'I fancy it's just what you and I have been doing for a good many years.' McTaggart worked mostly isolated from the 'art scene' and had little interest in the kind of theories that would label him 'impressionist' or even 'expressionist'. McTaggart was concerned to render movement in his paintings, using long flowing brushstrokes, and, unlike the Impressionists, often painted a turbulent nature.

James Guthrie, E. A. Hornel, John Lavery, W. Y. MacGregor, Alexander Roche and E. A. Walton. The chief foreign influences on their work were Gustave Courbet and the Barbizon painters of France, the Hague School of Holland, and most importantly in the early years, the Realist style of the French painter Jules Bastien-Lepage. He was enormously influential not only in France but also in Britain, and some of his best-known followers were those who formed a colony in Newlyn, Cornwall, under the leadership of Stanhope Forbes (see pages 15–18). Amongst the 'Glasgow Boys', Lavery had some instruction from Bastien-Lepage in 1883-4 while painting at Grez-sur-Loing, an established artists' colony near Fontainebleau.

Few of the new Glasgow painters concerned

themselves with the grim reality of industrial Glasgow. Their work was often frankly escapist or showed an interest in the rural landscape. E. A. Walton's *Berwickshire Field Workers* (1886), is a splendid example of the Glasgow style of the time, its subject matter and square brush strokes showing the evident influence of Bastien-Lepage. Walton painted in the early 1880s at Cockburnspath, a village a few miles south of Dunbar, just inland from the Berwickshire coast. The village became a summer colony for these artists, who painted the bleak life of the peasant workers in their austere landscape. In Walton's painting an upward-looking viewpoint is used to focus on a woman in clogs holding a scythe and wearing the protective cane and cotton headgear known as an 'ugly' which was characteristic of the area. There is a strange kind of inhumanity about this semi-masked woman standing rigid in her stark agricultural setting.

JOSEPH FARQUHARSON

By contrast with Walton's painting, the rural snowscapes of Joseph Farquharson present cold but attractively seasonal images which earned him great popular success during the same period. Farquharson was born in

JOSEPH FARQUHARSON

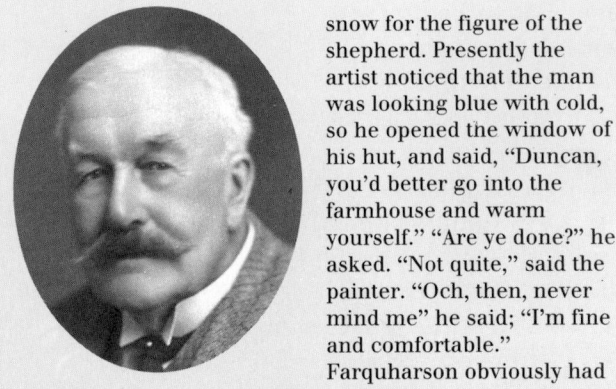

Joseph Farquharson 1847-1935

Joseph Farquharson, the nineteenth-century Scottish artist, mainly painted the Deeside area he had grown up in. He usually worked from within a movable hut he had constructed to protect him from the wintry weather, which became his speciality. An anecdote about *The Joyless Winter Day* tells how an old servant helped Farquharson with his paintings. 'Farquharson had him standing out in the snow for the figure of the shepherd. Presently the artist noticed that the man was looking blue with cold, so he opened the window of his hut, and said, "Duncan, you'd better go into the farmhouse and warm yourself." "Are ye done?" he asked. "Not quite," said the painter. "Och, then, never mind me" he said; "I'm fine and comfortable." Farquharson obviously had no 'servant problems'!

JOSEPH FARQUHARSON
The Joyless Winter Day
1883 Oil on canvas
104.1 × 180.3 cm
41 × 71 in

J. McINTOSH PATRICK
Winter in Angus
1935 Oil on canvas
75.6 × 101.6 cm
29¾ × 40 in

Aberdeenshire and became laird of Finzean, an estate between Balmoral and Aberdeen, inhabited by the artist's family since the sixteenth century. As a laird who took his position seriously, Farquharson was an expert on his land and wildlife as well as being a fine shot, though he did visit London regularly, where he had a studio, and was also a frequent contributor to Royal Academy exhibitions.

In 1883 Farquharson's *The Joyless Winter Day* made his name at the Academy when it was shown there. His understanding of Highland sheep was based on direct observation but those in his paintings derive from models made for him by William Wilson of Monymusk.

JAMES McINTOSH PATRICK

A twentieth-century inheritor of Farquharson's mantle as painter of Scottish snowscenes is James McIntosh Patrick. Patrick has spent most of his life painting the Angus landscape around Dundee, where he is a great celebrity and organizer of an annual summer open-air sketching class. As Scotland's best-known landscape painter today, Patrick creates a vision entirely different from those of his great predecessors. *Winter in Angus* (1935) is one of his greatest images, showing farm labourers at work at

Powrie Castle. The landscape is a composite one made from drawings done on the spot in the countryside near Dundee and then used in the artist's studio with its calm north light to create an exceptionally balanced composition. The extent to which Patrick's landscapes are invented can be gauged from his own comments on the painting *Winter in Angus*:

> *The castle came because I had already made a painting and an etching of Powrie Castle and I thought it would make a good subject for a big picture. But in* Winter in Angus *I created an imaginary viewpoint, up high. For the background – well, I wanted a complicated background and at that time I was teaching on Fridays at Glenalmond and the background is the view from the art room window which I fitted in behind the castle. I was looking for something for the foreground and I decided to put in the pigeon loft but apart from that the rest of the foreground is invented.*

Patrick used to rub down his initial painting and then rework the image into a sharp finish, thus increasing his distance from the original material yet ending with a realistic scene.

INDEX

ACKNOWLEDGEMENTS

The Publishers would like to thank the following organizations and individuals for their kind permission to reproduce the photographs in this book:
Andrew Besley Photo-Library: 15 top. John Bethell Photography: 35 bottom, 91, 92. Mary Evans Picture Library: 42 bottom left, 42 bottom right, 45 top, 66 top, 87 top, 88 bottom left, 88 bottom right, 108. John Glover: 144 top. Robert Harding Picture Library: 42 top, 129 right, /Trevor Wood 17. Highlands and Islands Development Board (Inverness) Photo Library: 166 top. The Hulton-Deutsch Collection: 23 left, 23 right, 52 top, 71 top, 149 top, 158 top. Jarrold, Norwich: 96 top. Landscape Only: 8-9, 32-3, 135 bottom, 159 top, 160-1. S and O Mathews Photography: 122-3. Colin Molyneux: 13 top. Clare Muller: 77. The National Gallery, London: 83 top. The National Portrait Gallery, London: 138 top, 171 top. The National Trust Photographic Library/J Whitaker: 38 top. Photos Great Britain: 78-9, 100 bottom. Pictures Colour Library: 56-7, 102-3. Scottish National Portrait Gallery, Edinburgh: 172 bottom. Swift Picture Library/David Oakes: 107. T D Timms Photography: 148 bottom. Judy Todd: 111 top, 167 top. Usher Gallery, Lincoln: 116. Andy Williams Photo Library: 51 bottom. Mike Williams Photography: 140-1. Jennie Woodcock: 133. Tim Woodcock: 29, 64 top.

All other material was supplied by The Tate Gallery, London.